Praise For

THE YOUNG MUSICIAN'S GUIDE TO SONGWRITING

"Lisa makes all aspects of songwriting (form, harmony, rhythm, lyrics, titles, etc.) amazingly easy in this book! Next time I do a songwriting class, it will be with Lisa's book!"

—Wendy Stevens, M.M., NCTM, composer, pianist, and teacher, www.composecreate.com

"As a successful songwriter and much–in–demand piano instructor who specializes in teaching children, Lisa was the perfect person to write this book. And the end result proves it: a treasure chest full of ideas, strategies, examples, and exercises that are bound to help and inspire kids and teachers alike.

In the section on musical styles, Lisa includes this quote by Oscar Wilde: "Be Yourself. Everyone else is already taken." And that's what her new book does—empowers each of us, through writing music and lyrics, to say what only we can say.

Thanks, Lisa, for filling this important need! I look forward to using *The Young Musician's Guide to Songwriting* with my own students."

—Bruce Siegel, private teacher and creator of DoctorKeys.com Piano Tutorials

"Lisa Donovan Lukas's book, *The Young Musician's Guide to Songwriting*, boils songwriting down into accessible, clear–cut blocks of information. Reading this book is like having a personal tutor at your side during your songwriting process.

I especially love how Lisa puts her own creative process on display for the benefit of the reader, displaying examples from her own songwriting experience.

Lisa, thank you for this invaluable resource!"

—Adam Bendorf, Founder of Alberti Publishing and independent music teacher, www.bendorfpianostudio.com

The Young Musician's Guide to Songwriting

How to Create Music and Lyrics

(For Music Students and Teachers)

For Charlie, Will, and Nathaniel — with all my best wishes! ♫

Lisa Donovan Lukas
Sept. 2014

The Young Musician's Guide to Songwriting

How to Create Music and Lyrics

(For Music Students and Teachers)

Lisa Donovan Lukas

MUST WRITE MUSIC, California

THE YOUNG MUSICIAN'S GUIDE TO SONGWRITING
How to Create Music and Lyrics
(For Music Students and Teachers)
By Lisa Donovan Lukas

Published by MUST WRITE MUSIC, California

For information please contact the author through the following website:
http://www.lisadonovanlukas.com

ISBN-13: 9780615915715

ISBN-10: 061591571X
Library of Congress Control Number: 2014900033
LCCN Imprint Name: Must Write Music, California

With special thanks to Ed ("Eddie Arms") Willumsen, my first piano teacher, who taught me to appreciate Bach, Mozart, Beethoven, Chopin, Debussy, Ravel, Schumann, Rodgers and Hart, Rodgers and Hammerstein, Burt Bacharach and Hal David, Leonard Bernstein, Stephen Sondheim, The Beatles, Joni Mitchell, Stevie Wonder, and Bob Dylan (to name just a very few, in no particular order)—and all at the same time.

I give additional thanks to my nephew, Harrison Long. He promised he would read this book for me and he kept his word, even in the face of his own practice schedule, band rehearsals, and late-night gigs! I very much appreciated his input and perspective.

~ Support Our Young Creators ~
10% of all author royalties are donated to music educational not-for-profits, including The Music Teachers' Association of California Foundation and Westside Music Foundation

(Piano lessons—back in the day—with "Eddie Arms")

This book is dedicated to my husband and treasured friend Ron, to my most loved son, Jack – and to my mother and father, who got me started with music and lyrics and fanned the flames every step of the way.

CONTENTS

1

LET'S GET STARTED

"Imagination is the key to my lyrics. The rest is painted with a little science fiction...All I'm writing is just what I feel, that's all."
—Jimi Hendrix

"I tend to be a subscriber to the idea that you have everything you need by the time you're 12 years old to do interesting writing for most of the rest of your life—certainly by the time you're 18."
—Bruce Springsteen

HELLO...

This book is for kids who read music and play an instrument really well and for kids who are just beginning to learn an instrument. It's also for kids who might be someplace in the middle of these two scenarios.

Whether you're an accomplished musician, or just starting out; whether you have musical training, read music, and play an instrument; whether you're just getting your feet wet; or whether you stand somewhere in between, now is the time to begin if you want to write your own material.

Why is it a good time to begin? If you want to learn and have something to say, you can write a song. Maybe you've seen other kids write songs and wondered: "Can I?" Well, I'm going to say, you can!

Have you ever wondered how to write songs? Maybe you are:

1. A terrific musician and have studied your instrument for quite a few years—maybe even longer.
2. Just beginning to learn an instrument and your future feels bright with all that possibility.
3. Somewhere in the middle of those two scenarios.

Maybe you've written some tunes before, or maybe you've always just sort of wondered how to get down to it. Either which way, you've got some creative energy, musical interests, and the desire to write your own material.

This is the perfect time to crack open my book on songwriting and take a look around. At any rate, I want to welcome you to my guide dedicated to the creation of words and music for young people.

Personally, I think you're in for a lot of fun! And, if this grabs you, you just might be in for more than a lifetime of magic and beyond.

If you want to express yourself in song, you can learn to write both music and lyrics. If you don't want to write both, you can find a partner. For example, your partner might work on music while you create lyrics, or vice versa.

Maybe you're a terrific musician and have spent years playing other people's music—and now you want to create some of your own. Or maybe you're just beginning to learn an instrument and want to express yourself in song.

> Are you an accomplished musician who plays other people's music most of the time? Do you want to try writing your own?

Maybe you're a poet but never thought about writing a song. Are you worried that you can't come up with lyrics?

BTW: You can use these ideas if you're older too. I won't stop you. Really.

> What if I'm not a kid? It's okay, it's not too late! The tools I give you here will work for you too.

So, how does this work and why this book?

> I will give you:
>
> - Ways to begin quickly
> - Easy-to-use ideas
> - Methods to jumpstart songs
> - Techniques for accomplished musicians as well as beginners
> - A step-by-step approach, so you can pick up wherever you are
> - Guidance for anyone with something to say
> - Exercises from basic to advanced
> - Lessons to create structure, lyrics, melody, harmony, and rhythm

Whatever level you're at and whatever kind of learner you are, I have a pathway in for you. With simple step-by-step guidance, you will be writing your own songs.

Important side notes:

If you're just getting going with learning an instrument and reading music, don't worry. You can still work this out and start from where you are. As you learn more about music and acquire more skills with your instrument, you can always revisit some of my exercises with chords and harmony. *And if you hang on to this book long enough, after a while, you will find different things in it that speak to you at different times on your musical path.*

Meanwhile, you might:

1. Find that you have a great melodic sense.
2. Collaborate with another writer who knows chords and harmony already.
3. Create the tune and have someone else show you how to write it down and/or help you decide on the chords.
4. Write the lyrics and collaborate with someone else who will write the music.

Musical Factoid:

- One of the greatest American songwriters of all time was Irving Berlin.
- He did not read music and was a self-taught pianist.
- He even played most of the time in the key of F sharp so that he could stay mainly on the black keys!
- George Gershwin said that Irving Berlin was one of the all time greatest songwriters that ever lived (and George Gershwin would know ☺).
- Berlin wrote approximately 1500 songs in his lifetime, and many of his songs became major hits.
- Some of Berlin's songs were nominated for Academy Awards.

Personally, I think that if you learn all you can about music, it will only contribute to your creativity and to the quality and quantity of your material. The more you know, the more you can control your creations. Also, the more you will be inspired.

Maybe you practice with your instrument one day to work on scales, harmony, or a piece. You make a mistake and miss a note. Then you think: Hey, that's nice—that sounds good to my ear! Sometimes mistakes can turn into inspiration. This mistake could be the beginning of a new song. Then again, maybe not! Maybe you just want to practice some more to get the notes right! ☺

One of my piano and songwriting students was worried because she thought that if she learned to read music and understand music theory, it might interfere with her creativity. My belief is that the more technique and knowledge you can master, the better. Everything you take in, every skill you have, contributes to your ability to create.

But we all have to start somewhere.

> This isn't "One Size Fits All." You are unique, and the path you choose will be unique too.

I heard somewhere recently that when Paul McCartney from The Beatles was a kid, he used to take the chords from Rodgers and Hart songs and write his own new melodies and lyrics to those chords. If that's true, it makes perfect sense to me because it's a wonderful way to learn how to write songs. It's just one way, but it's a really good one!

Speaking of Paul McCartney, let's talk a little bit about learning from the greats.

LEARN FROM THE MASTERS...

Now. We've got *amazing* singer-songwriter performers—like say, Carole King, Bob Dylan, Paul Simon, Billy Joel, Stevie Wonder, and Joni Mitchell, just to name a few. They have their own style, their own voice. They write both music and lyrics and perform their own material. Other people may eventually cover their tunes, but still, when we hear these original songwriters, we know who they are right off the bat.

Kurt Cobain was a wonderful singer-songwriter, guitarist, and performer. He wrote the lyrics and collaborated with his band Nirvana on the music. Alanis Morissette writes and performs her own material as well. Some of her early albums are songwriting collaborations, and some of her later material is all Alanis Morissette—both words and music. She has the ability to write on her own and to collaborate as well.

In addition to singer/songwriter/performers, we have other kinds of songwriters:

1. Some songwriters do not necessarily perform or even play an instrument all that well. (Remember Irving? We're not going to quibble with Irving, right?) These songwriters may write songs for musicals or songs for other people to cover.

2. Some songwriters are writing teams like Rodgers and Hart, Rodgers and Hammerstein, Barry Mann and Cynthia Weil, Burt Bacharach and Hal David, and Eric Lowen and Dan Navarro.

3. Others write *both* music and lyrics for other people, such as Diane Warren, Stephen Schwartz, Stephen Sondheim (who also wrote lyrics for Leonard Bernstein's music), and Cole Porter.

4. Then there are bands with writing members like The Beatles, Coldplay, Eagles, The Beachboys, Grateful Dead, OneRepublic, Linkin Park, U2, Blink-182, and on and on—lots of combinations!

5. We also have songwriter/performers like Elton John, who perform and sing and write the music for someone else's lyrics (Bernie Taupin's lyrics, in Elton John's case.)

Songwriting is a deep and vast subject. There's structure and form to consider, as well as lyrics, melody, harmony, and rhythm. There's also performance, recording, demoing, leadsheets, computer programs, arranging, and the coordination of other players. There's the whole business aspect of songwriting too.

What I want to address in my guide is not the commercial, or the recording and producing aspects. I want to talk about the principles involved in the creative process of songwriting.

There are certain techniques that you can practice and develop. As you hone your abilities, you begin to communicate with song. And this is really fun. Really, really fun.

CONCEPTS...

You might wonder: "How do I come up with concepts for songs?"; "How do I even begin to actually write a song?"; or "What should I write about?"

There are many different ways to go. Let's start with a list of basic emotions and then apply them to some of the different situations below to see how they might lead to a few ideas for songs.

Some of our more fundamental emotions are:

1. Love
2. Joy
3. Anger
4. Sadness
5. Surprise
6. Fear
7. Trust

One way to go is to bring some basic human feelings into play (and take your pick, 'cause we've got lots of them to choose from!) with a scenario that is happening during a certain time frame: for example, something that will (or might) happen *someday* ("Angel" by Sarah McLachlan or "The Times They Are a-Changin" by Bob Dylan), a situation that's happening *now* ("Apologize" by Ryan Tedder of OneRepublic, "We Belong" by Lowen and Navarro, "Thunder Road" by Bruce Springsteen), or something that has already happened sometime *before* ("Blue Moon" by Richard Rodgers and Lorenz Hart or "Bad Day" by Daniel Powter).

You can also think about applying some of these basic human emotions to the following scenarios for some more song ideas:

1. YOUR OWN REAL STORY: Give us specific details in a story about your own life. Make it real, yet something we can all relate to (for example, "California" by Joni Mitchell).

2. IMAGINARY/INVENTED PERSONAS/CHARACTERS: You can pretend to be someone else (from a story or novel? from a movie? from the news? from history? from your family or friends?) ("Highwayman" by Jimmy Webb or "Ziggy Stardust" by David Bowie). What is the character feeling? —Maybe sadness, maybe fear, or maybe joy?

3. LOVE SONGS: There are so many different situations and feelings that go with love. Here are a number of various kinds of love songs:

    a. SEARCHING FOR LOVE (for example, "Lookin' for Love" by Wanda Mallette, Patti Ryan, and Bob Morrison; "Somebody to Love" by Freddie Mercury of Queen)

b. BEING IN LOVE (for example, "Love Story" by Taylor Swift; "Teenage Dream" by Katy Perry, Lukasz Gottwald, Max Martin, Benjamin Levin, and Bonnie McKee; "Evergreen" by Barbra Streisand and Paul Williams; "Endless Love" by Lionel Ritchie)

c. LOVE, LIKE IT ONCE WAS (for example, "You've Lost That Lovin' Feelin'" by Barry Mann, Phil Spector, and Cynthia Weil; "The Boys of Summer" lyrics by Don Henley and music by Don Henley and Mike Campbell)

d. LOSING LOVE (for example, "A Thousand Miles" by Vanessa Carlton; "On a Bus to St. Cloud" by Gretchen Peters; "I'll Never Love This Way Again" by Richard Kerr (music) and Will Jennings (lyrics); "Ain't No Sunshine" by Bill Withers)

e. BREAKING UP (for example, "Someone Like You" by Adele and Dan Wilson; "By the Time I Get to Phoenix" by Jimmy Webb)

4. A SONG TOLD LIKE A STORY OR FOLKTALE: Sometimes these songs can be created as first-person narratives (for example, "Ode to Billie Joe" by Bobbie Gentry).

5. DANCE SONGS: (for example, "Jungle Boogie" by Kool and the Gang; "Rhythm of the Night" by Corona; "Get Into the Groove" by Madonna and Steve Bray; "Caribbean Queen" by Billy Ocean)

6. FUNNY DANCE SONGS: Humorous music that gives us lessons for certain dances ("Macarena" by Los del Rio; "The Locomotion" by Gerry Goffin and Carole King; "YMCA" by Jacques Morali, Henri Belolo, and Victor Willis; "The Hustle" by

Van McCoy; "The Cha Cha Slide" created by DJ Casper; or "Achy Breaky Heart" by Don Von Tress). Maybe it's the emotion of joy that is also involved in songs like these.

7. COMEDY SONGS: ("Rocky Raccoon" by Lennon/McCartney; "Adelaide's Lament" from *Guys and Dolls* by Frank Loesser) There is a fine line between comedy and tragedy! (For parody songs, you can listen to songs by Weird Al Yankovic.)

8. PHILOSOPHICAL IDEAS AND MESSAGES: These give us something we can all understand and identify with (for example, "The Living Years" by Mike Rutherford and B.A. Robertson).

> Your own life, books you've read, or movies you've seen are also excellent sources of inspiration. Write down your ideas as you move through your life. You can come up with material for songs from your own life and from the things that influence you and that touch you.

More ways to come up with ideas:

1. Observe. Be a people watcher!
2. Pay attention to conversations/dialogue.
3. Find unique ideas from the world around you, the world you live in.
4. Read the newspaper, go to movies, museums, read books and poetry.
5. Keep a journal/notebook/diary. (whatever works for you! ☺)

6. Take situations from your own life and write about them.

7. Write down your dreams when you wake up in the morning. You might be able to find some songs in them.

If you experiment with all or even some of these ideas, you will have plenty of things to write about.

JOURNALS...

Your own genuine situations contain wonderful material for songwriting. You can write what you know. When something is real, it moves people.

Add these things together to reach other people:

1. Real Life
2. Words
3. Music

Your musical style:

1. If you don't like rock and roll, rap, or folk music, for example, you don't have to write it!

"Be yourself; everyone else is already taken." Oscar Wilde ~ Irish writer & poet

2. Aim for what you are attracted to.

3. Be yourself.

However! If something interests you and you don't know *how* to write it:

1. Listen to see what's going on.

2. Figure out what's happening musically and lyrically, and then see if you can do it too! (I bet you can. ☺)

Songs can:

1. Create positive advances in the world
2. Help us become more aware
3. Shake things up and move people
4. Encourage empathy and promote kindness
5. Reach out and communicate with people
6. Make us think

THINKING ABOUT TITLES...

With songwriting the title and the idea go hand in hand. But even though they're tied together, they aren't exactly the same.

For instance, Joni Mitchell's "The Circle Game" talks about the passing of time, different stages of our lives, and how we can't turn back the clock. How we can only go forward. But, wouldn't those two whole long sentences make a terrible title for a song? ☺

(Oh, I want to play you my new song. It's called: "The passing of time, and different stages of our lives, and how we can't turn back the clock, we can only move ahead in time." LOL)

> Titles are much shorter than the whole idea. They can be catchy and they can encapsulate that whole idea or concept in just a few words or sometimes in one or two words (i.e. "The Circle Game").

Okay! Let's say we have a great concept for a song. All right...so now what? How can we take our concept and turn it into an actual song?

BEGINNINGS...

Here are some different ways to go:

1. If you write the lyrics, you can work with a partner who will write the music. If you write the music, you can work with a partner who will write the words. Maybe you will both work on music and lyrics at the same time, together, as a team. If you write both music and lyrics on your own, you might write a melody and then afterward, create the lyrics to go with it. Or, you might write the words first. Experiment!

2. Create a groove using a sequencing program (such as GarageBand, Logic, Performer, or whatever sequencing program you like best), and when you're done, invent some words spontaneously in the moment by improvising.

3. Work at the piano (or whatever instrument you use) and improvise. Go for whatever comes to mind. Find the groove of the music and make up some lyrics as you go. You can refine everything afterward.

4. Write many different versions of your song (music, words, or both.) Work things out as you keep changing and revising.

5. "Automatic" journal writing: put down everything and anything that jumps to mind without editing or second guessing. When you're done writing freely, start sifting through your material for ideas and images that go together to help you construct your actual lyrics. (This one is my particular favorite!)

There is no *one* way to do it. There is no right or wrong way to begin. Experiment with the list above. Use these different techniques to get started. See what works for you and what you come up with!

HELPFUL TOOLS OF THE TRADE...

With all of these different creative approaches to try, you might also really enjoy having:

1. A thesaurus: a book that lists words and groups them together according to their similarity. It provides synonyms (similar words) and antonyms (opposite words.) I like *Roget's International Thesaurus of English Words and Phrases*. I also like to use: http://thesaurus.com/

2. A rhyming dictionary: a special dictionary used when writing lyrics and poetry with organized lists of words that rhyme. I like to use *The Complete Rhyming Dictionary and Poet's Craft Book* by Clement Wood. I also like to use: http://www.rhymezone.com

More inspiration:

Take notes! You can go on a search for books, articles, and information having to do with the chosen topic for your song. You can use magazines, newspapers, Google, and your local library to get motivated and energized.

> A thesaurus, a rhyming dictionary, your own notes: these are fantastic *tools of the trade!*

HISTORY'S HEAVYWEIGHT SONGS...

> Get motivated to write your own unique songs by listening to some of the greatest songs that are already out there!

Excellent writing is often inspired by excellent writing. As creators, fresh out of the gate, we walk behind the heavyweights who came before us.

So. If you like pop, rock, country, musicals, or blues, it's from the mighty influences of whatever thing you resonate with that you can eventually develop and create your own voice, style, and originality.

BB King: "I don't think anybody steals anything; all of us borrow."

Get inspired. Pick out some songs you absolutely *love* and figure out what's going on. What about them grabs you? Let the answers to that question guide you.

Pay attention to the fantastic talents that came down the pike before you. Learn from them and let them help you become who *you* are in your own songs.

New sculptors, painters, and composers imitate the pros and virtuosos when they first learn to sculpt, paint, or compose. Later on, they develop their own style. You can do the same thing. You can learn from the amazing songwriters and composers in history and allow them to help you grow. Then express yourself in your own unique way, with your own voice.

Take a look at my list of songs at the end of this chapter. These songs are off the top of my head. It would be impossible to include everything because there's so much greatness out there! And since that's the case, I decided to make a list of some of my favorite songs, coming up through the eras.

Of course, everyone has his/her own preferences. These are some of mine.

Keep in mind that great new songs are being written all the time, every minute. So already, my song lists here are missing amazing new material! The important thing is to keep listening and appreciating.

EXERCISE:

1. Feel free to take a listen and explore these songs along your way.
2. Make your own lists of favorite songs, favorite songwriters, favorite bands, and performers.
3. Refer to your list of favorites as we explore different exercises throughout this songwriting guide.

(Let's just think of this as our jumping off point! Of course, this is just the tip of the iceberg.)

A FEW FAVORITE SONGS FROM A FEW FAVORITE SONGWRITERS OF MINE...

Cole Porter

1. "I've Got You Under My Skin"
2. "Just One of Those Things"
3. "I Get a Kick Out of You"

George and Ira Gershwin:

1. "Someone to Watch Over Me"

2. “Let’s Call the Whole Thing Off”
3. “Embraceable You”
4. “A Foggy Day”

Richard Rodgers and Lorenz Hart

1. “Blue Moon”
2. “My Funny Valentine”
3. “My Romance”
4. “You Took Advantage of Me”

Richard Rodgers and Oscar Hammerstein II

1. “If I Loved You”
2. “I Whistle a Happy Tune”
3. “My Favorite Things”
4. “Edelweiss”
5. “Do-Re-Mi”

Irving Berlin

1. "Cheek to Cheek"
2. "Puttin' on the Ritz"
3. "There's No Business Like Show Business"

Dorothy Fields and Jerome Kern

1. "The Way You Look Tonight"

Dorothy Fields and Jimmy McHugh

1. "I Can't Give You Anything but Love"
2. "On the Sunny Side of the Street"

Burt Bacharach and Hal David

1. "I Say a Little Prayer"
2. "Walk On By"
3. "I'll Never Fall in Love Again"
4. "Odds and Ends"

Barry Mann and Cynthia Weil

1. "You've Lost That Lovin' Feelin" (also with Phil Spector)
2. "Somewhere Out There" (also with James Horner)
3. "Here You Come Again"
4. "Just Once"
5. "Never Gonna' Let You Go"

Stephen Sondheim

1. "Send in the Clowns"
2. "Johanna"
3. "Not While I'm Around"
4. "Pretty Women"
5. "Tonight" (lyrics for Leonard Bernstein's music/*Westside Story*)
6. "America" (lyrics for Leonard Bernstein's music/*Westside Story*)

(Also, check out Sondheim's musicals: *Company, A Little Night Music, Sweeney Todd,* and more!)

The Beatles (songs written mainly by John Lennon/Paul McCartney, but also a number by George Harrison and sometimes Ringo Starr)

1. "Please Please Me"
2. "Hold Me Tight"
3. "If I Fell"
4. "I Should Have Known Better"
5. "Can't Buy Me Love"
6. "I'll Follow the Sun"
7. "It's Only Love"
8. "Let It Be"
9. "Nowhere Man"
10. "Here, There and Everywhere"
11. "With a Little Help from My Friends"
12. "I Will"
13. "Julia"
14. "All You Need Is Love"
15. "Rocky Raccoon"

16. "Octopus's Garden"
17. "Yesterday"

(and many more!)

Bob Dylan

1. "Like a Rolling Stone"
2. "Mr. Tambourine Man"
3. "Just Like a Woman"
4. "Lay Lady Lay"

(and many more!)

Paul Simon

1. "The Sound of Silence"
2. "Bridge over Troubled Water"
3. "Mrs. Robinson"
4. "The Boy in the Bubble" (music written with Forere Motloheloa)
5. "Graceland"

(and many more!)

Jimmy Webb

1. "Up, Up and Away"
2. "By the Time I Get to Phoenix"
3. "The Moon Is a Harsh Mistress"
4. "Highwayman"
5. "Galveston"
6. "Wichita Lineman"
7. "MacArthur Park"

(and many more!)

The Eagles (most songs by: Glenn Frey/Don Henley/Don Felder)

1. "One of These Nights" (Henley/Frey)
2. "Desperado" (Henley/Frey)
3. "Hotel California"
4. "Best of My Love" (Don Henley, Glenn Frey and J.D. Souther)

Michael Jackson:

1. "Bad"

2. "Beat It"

3. "Billie Jean"

Don Henley

1. "The Boys of Summer" (music: Henley, Mike Campbell; lyrics: Henley)

2. "The End of the Innocence" (Don Henley, Bruce Hornsby)

Carole King

1. "Tapestry"

2. "I Feel the Earth Move"

3. "You've Got a Friend"

Joni Mitchell

1. "Both Sides Now"

2. "Big Yellow Taxi"

3. "Circle Game"

4. "Ladies of the Canyon"

5. "You Turn Me On I'm a Radio"

6. "Raised on Robbery"
7. "For the Roses"
8. "Little Green"

(and many, many more!)

Carly Simon

1. "Anticipation"
2. "You're So Vain"
3. "You Belong to Me" (Carly Simon, Michael McDonald)
4. "The Right Thing to Do"

(and many more!)

James Taylor

1. "Fire and Rain"
2. "Carolina in My Mind"

Cat Stevens

1. "Father and Son"
2. "Wild World"

3. "Peace Train"

4. "Moon Shadow"

Stevie Wonder

1. "My Cherie Amour"

2. "You Are the Sunshine of My Life"

3. "Superstition"

4. "I Just Called to Say I Love You"

(and *many* more!)

Randy Newman

1. "I Love L.A."

2. "Short People"

3. "Rednecks"

Dolly Parton

1. "Coat of Many Colors"

2. "Jolene"

3. "I Will Always Love You"
4. "9 to 5"

Elton John and Bernie Taupin

1. "Crocodile Rock"
2. "Your Song"
3. "Tiny Dancer"
4. "Rocket Man"

(and *many* more!)

Billy Joel

1. "Just the Way You Are"
2. "She's Always a Woman"
3. "Uptown Girl"
4. "Piano Man"

(and *many* more!)

Diane Warren

1. "How Do I Live"

2. "If You Asked Me To"

3. "Love Will Lead You Back"

4. "When I'm Back on My Feet Again"

More Favorite Songwriters:

Jackson Browne
Bruce Springsteen
Elvis Costello
J.D. Souther
Laura Nyro
Neil Young
Eric Clapton
Sting
Dan Fogelberg
Lowen and Navarro
Buddy Holly
Gretchen Peters
Lionel Richie
Tracy Chapman
Bruce Hornsby
Alanis Morissette and Glen Ballard
Daniel Powter
Sarah McLachlan
Natalie Merchant
Loreena McKennitt
Tori Amos

Taylor Swift
Adele
Vanessa Carlton
Skip Ewing
Sheryl Crow
Seal
Jewel
The Milk Carton Kids (Joey Ryan and Kenneth Pattengale)
Stephen Schwartz
Robert Lopez

Rap/Hip-Hop:

Biggie Smalls
Jay-Z
Snoop Dogg
Tupac Shakur (2Pac)

More Bands and More Inspiration:

The Beach Boys
Grateful Dead
The Eagles
The Police
The Rolling Stones
Linkin Park
Coldplay
U2
Crosby, Stills and Nash
Fleetwood Mac
Steely Dan
Led Zeppelin
AC/DC
Nirvana

Sex Pistols
Cream
The Allman Brothers Band
Jimi Hendrix
Stevie Ray Vaughn
Queen
Regina Spektor
Muse
The Strokes
Green Day
The Killers
Franz Ferdinand
Blink 182
Flogging Molly
Radiohead

More:

"Airplanes"—B.o.B.
"California Gurls"—Katy Perry (and Snoop Dogg)
"Billionaire"—Travie McCoy
"Not Afraid"—Eminem
"Rock That Body"—Black Eyed Peas

Also...more faves (songs covered in the 40's and 50's):

"When You Wish Upon A Star"—Leigh Harline and Ned Washington
"Route 66"—Bobby Troup
"All Or Nothing At All"—by Arthur Altman and Jack Lawrence
"As Time Goes By"—Herman Hupfeld
"All I Have to Do Is Dream"—Felice and Boudleaux Bryant
"Bye Bye Love"—Felice and Boudleaux Bryant
"Rock Around the Clock"—Max C. Freedman and Jimmy De Knight

"Smoke Gets In Your Eyes"—Jerome Kern and Otto Harbach
"Put Your Head On My Shoulder"—Paul Anka
"Cry Me a River"—Arthur Hamilton

2
SONG STRUCTURE

"It was my 16th birthday—my mom and dad gave me my Goya classical guitar that day. I sat down, wrote this song, and I just knew that that was the only thing I could ever really do—write songs and sing them to people."
—Stevie Nicks

"I have a love for simple basic song structure, although sometimes you'd never know it."
—Laura Nyro

What are the elements that comprise a song? How do we put those elements together?

> The essence of songwriting takes the following ingredients and mixes them all together: structure, melody, lyric, rhyme, repetition, harmony, rhythm, and the title of the song. My plan is to talk about each of these elements in my book, one by one.

I'm going to start with the structure because that's the foundation; that's where the house gets built. And just like we have different types of houses (mediterranean, craftsman, traditional, modern, etc.), we have a number of different structures at our disposal that we can choose from in order to build our songs.

> The way a song is organized is known as structure. It's also called form. Structure is:
>
> 1. Where and how the verses, choruses, intros, pre-choruses, and bridges are constructed and then arranged within the song.
> 2. The separate sections of a song that are assembled together so that each section flows naturally into the next.

Okay. Let's take a look at song structure up close.

When we get down to it, we find that pretty much all the songs we know and love are built using just a few particular forms. You can find this out for yourself very easily. Begin to keep track of things when you listen to songs. This is easy and fun to do, and I'll show you how in these next exercises. (If you're just starting out with music, you might choose to start with the "Exercise For Newer Musicians" coming up ahead.)

EXERCISE:

1. Choose a song in 4/4 time to start.
2. After the intro (usually 4 to 8 bars), begin by listening to the first vocal section of the song. We'll call this A.
3. Number (as in write this down!) and keep track of the beats and measures from the very beginning of the melody (e.g. 1, 2, 3, 4; 2, 2, 3, 4; 3, 2, 3, 4; 4, 2, 3, 4; and so on).
4. Keep track of your measures until you come to the next musical section (contrasting idea). We'll call this B.
5. Figure out the number of bars in this new B section.
6. Do this for each section, starting with bar one, for each section.
7. Keep track of all these various contrasting sections. They are called verses, pre-choruses, choruses, bridges, and/or instrumental solos—and I will explain each of these in more detail just a little bit more down the road here.
8. Meanwhile, while you're beginning to calculate the bars, just label each section with the letters of the alphabet, starting with A and moving through the alphabet with each contrasting section.
9. When you hear the same music play again, label that new section with the same letter you marked it as initially.

You might get a little "alphabet chart" that resembles this:

A—8
B—8
A—8
B—8
C—4
B—8

Or maybe this:

A—8
A—8
B—8
Instrumental—4
A—8

EXERCISE:

1. Do the above exercise for three or four (or more!) songs.
2. You'll start seeing similarities for sure! And even though you will see repeating forms, you will discover differences in them as well. There might be some extra bars or other little alterations too that make each tune unique.

EXERCISE FOR NEWER MUSICIANS:

1. Listen to a favorite song a number of times and see if you can get a hold of the rhythmic feel.
2. After a few times through, see if you can start to identify the contrasting sections of the song and where those changes start to occur.
3. Write down A for the first section, and when you hear a new and different sounding section, write down B. When you hear the song return to the first section, write down A again. If you hear something completely new, that will be C, and so forth (and if you hear the second section repeat again, then that's B again, etc.).
4. You will find that patterns emerge.
5. If you do this exercise with a few songs, you will start to see similar forms.
6. After you've gone through a few songs in this way, take a look at the first two exercises and see if you can identify sections by counting as well.

Now you can listen very closely to some of your favorite songs. Take those songs apart and analyze them according to the principals on form that you read about here. Then you can see for yourself how the songs you really like have been built. After a while, you will notice that there are only a few forms for songs that are used over and over again.

You can even start to do this anywhere you are. You might be in the car with the radio on...Let your mind count bars and listen to the melody and chord changes to see which song structure is being used! You can do it while you watch a movie or a TV show when a main title (or end credit) song is on. Or, put your headphones on and listen to iTunes. See how many song structures you can figure out.

Something more to keep in mind! There are two ways to view structure:

1. The overall structure of our composition (such as ABAB, etc.) and...
2. The harmonic structure (the chord progressions we decide to use). We will cover that more in the chapter on harmony.

Sometimes an artist/singer/songwriter will stray from these standard forms, but basically, the majority of songs will use one of these structures:

1. VERSE, VERSE, BRIDGE, VERSE: A, A, B, A

(With the first structure, there is no chorus and the title can work really well in the last line of each verse).

2. VERSE, CHORUS, VERSE, CHORUS: A,B,A,B

3. VERSE, CHORUS, VERSE, CHORUS, VERSE, CHORUS: A,B,A,B,A,B

4. VERSE, CHORUS, VERSE, CHORUS, BRIDGE, CHORUS: A,B,A,B,C,B

5. VERSE, VERSE, CHORUS, VERSE, CHORUS, CHORUS: A,A,B,A,B,B

6. VERSE, PRE-CHORUS, CHORUS, VERSE, PRE-CHORUS, CHORUS:
   A, A1, B, A, A1, B – (at times, with a BRIDGE as well)

Sometimes there are variations on these structures. You can listen and count to see where they happen. But that being said, these are the fundamental time-honored forms that you can use as templates to create your own original material.

We can try to use these patterns in imaginative and creative ways. They are compelling devices, and we can take advantage of them in order to communicate with our songs.

Here are some examples of pop songs that represent a number of these very common song-form structures:

1. ABAB: "Change the World" (Tommy Sims /Gordon Kennedy/ Wayne Kirkpatrick)

2. ABABCB: "Love Will Lead You Back" (Diane Warren)
   "Tracks of My Tears" (Smokey Robinson, Pete Moore, Marv Tarplin)
   "If You Asked Me To" (Diane Warren)

3. ABABAB: "Circle Game" (Joni Mitchell)
   "Candle in the Wind" (Elton John, Bernie Taupin)

4. AABA: "Will You Still Love Me Tomorrow" (Gerry Goffin, Carole King)
   "Saving All My Love for You (Michael Masser, Gerry Goffin)
   "The Way We Were" (Marilyn and Alan Bergman, Marvin Hamlisch)

Popular songs are built by combining:

1. VERSES
2. PRE-CHORUSES
3. CHORUSES
4. BRIDGES

VERSE:

The verse is the place to express the song's story. The verse will then lead to the chorus or the pre-chorus, depending on the ultimate structure of the song. If the song has no chorus, the verse may have the title—usually at the end of the verse.

Because the verse gives us facts that guide us to the title of the song, it is where the listener gets to know the story and first meets everyone involved: the protagonists, the heroes, the angels, or the villains. The verse holds all the specifics (the meat and potatoes!) and the basic activity of the song.

Here are some interesting things to know about verses:

1. Every verse of the song will have the same (or basically the same) tune with different words. The lyrics in each verse will convey new material.

2. Each line will share the exact same (or close to the same) number of syllables (for example: The 1st line of the 1st verse will have

the exact number of syllables as the 1st line of the 2nd verse, etc.) That way, we can sing the same melody for each verse.

3. The rhyme schemes will also match. For instance, if the 2nd and 4th lines of the first verse rhyme, the 2nd and 4th lines of the second verse will rhyme as well, and so on.

4. Normally, songs with a chorus won't have the title in the verse.

5. The verse will (hopefully) lead naturally to the chorus or to the pre-chorus.

PRE-CHORUS:

A *pre-chorus* can be used to create tension.

Not all songs will have a pre-chorus, but if they do, it will come right before the chorus so that it leads right into the chorus. This helps to create interest and can keep the song from becoming too repetitious.

Here are some interesting things to know about pre choruses:

1. Normally, the pre-chorus is a 2 or 4 line section (or even just 1 to 2 lyric lines) right before we go into the chorus; (they can sometimes be a little longer, but this is just generally speaking.)

2. The main function is to take (lift!) us to the chorus.

3. The pre-chorus is not mandatory—but if a song has one in the 1st verse, it will also appear in the following verses, in the exact same spot.

4. The melodic line of all the pre-choruses will be identical (or basically identical.) They can also use identical words, or brand new words. But usually, the words will be the same—or nearly the same.

CHORUS:

> The chorus encapsulates what the song is about in a more all-encompassing, universal way than the verse. The chorus also emphasizes the title of the song.

The chorus will contain the "hooky" tune. It's what we might call "hooky" because it hooks us right in and makes us want to sing out loud!

The chorus will express the basic meaning and emotion of the song. It has memorable melodies and lyric lines. This is the part of the song we all can't stop remembering or singing, even if we really want to!

> Have you ever tried to fall asleep at night but couldn't because a song kept repeating and repeating in your head? It was probably the chorus! (Or, it was at least one of the more "hooky" parts of the song's chorus.)

Think: "Chorus" = simple + catchy! ☺

> The verses hold the specific information: the story, the characters.
>
> The chorus is more general and conveys the primary emotion of the song.

Here are some interesting things to know about choruses:

1. We hear the title at least once in the chorus and often more than once.

2. The chorus contains the same melody every time it repeats, normally with the same lyrics.

3. Even though the lyrics are the same every time the chorus repeats, there's room for variation, so sometimes there is a little different lyric for an extra-meaningful last chorus.

THE TITLE IN A VERSE/CHORUS SONG:

In a verse/chorus song, the title is found in the chorus and it's the title that often repeats as well. If we repeat other lines, then the listener will be confused and wonder what the title is.

> The title is often set to a simple melodic line, something easy to sing.

The title can be repeated a number of times in the chorus, and there are many different ways you can choose to do this. In other words, there aren't really strict "rules" about where to put your title. It can be in the first line, or in the last line. It can repeat a number of times, or it can be in all of the lines of the chorus. Experiment and see what you like. The sky is really the limit!

Of course, there are always wonderful and interesting departures. The song title "Smells Like Teen Spirit" (Nirvana) doesn't appear in the song at all!

THE BRIDGE:

The bridge is an escape from the main foundation of the song. An important purpose of the bridge is to bring the song up a notch and to give additional meaning to the song as well. It will then guide us back to the chorus again, but this time, there's a new way of looking at things—a different perception.

Here are some interesting things to know about bridges:

1. Since the bridge normally appears only once in the song, it will have it's own unique melody (contrasting from both the verse and chorus).

2. With verse/chorus formats, the bridge will be between the 2nd and the 3rd chorus (i.e., ABABCB).

3. The bridge gives us another view in the song's narrative and a chance to head back into the chorus with new, heightened meaning.

4. The title is not ordinarily used in the bridge.

5. Sometimes the bridge can be instrumental (no lyrics–just a solo)

6. Sometimes, the bridge is very short and sweet–just enough to provide some contrast before the chorus is repeated for the last time (or the last couple of times).

7. Not all songs have, or need, a bridge (except in AABA forms, where the B *is* the Bridge).

The following are some devices you can apply to the music and lyrics to create a contrasting bridge section in your songs:

1. Rhythmic alteration

2. Use some new chords

3. If the melody is varied before, try the use of repeated notes. (The key is contrast!)

4. Change the range of the melody

5. Go from universal, broad ideas to more precise, descriptive ideas (or the other way around!)

6. Present another feature to your song's plot

7. Head into the future (or the past) if the song takes place now (or other changes of chronology)

8. Alter the point of view of the character (she/he/I/me/you)

9. Introduce a new twist or turn in the story

How can we create interest, tension, and contrast?

1. Build the verse and chorus using different grooves/rhythmic feel.
2. Use different chord progressions in the verse and in the chorus (also for the bridge if you have one).
3. Alter the melody in the different sections of the song.
4. If the verse is wordy, make the chorus sparse, or vice versa.
5. Make the words feel genuine, like the way we speak in conversation and everyday exchanges with people.

EXERCISE:

Choose some songs on your song list. Take a look at:

1. Form
2. The Title
3. Verses, Pre-Choruses (if any), Choruses, Bridges (if any)
4. Is there a pre-chorus? If so, how many measures?
5. Is there a bridge? If so, how does the writer differentiate the bridge from the rest of the sections? (lyrically? musically?)
6. How does the chorus differ from the verse?
7. Count how many measures are in each of the following sections: intro, verse, pre-chorus (if there is one), chorus, bridge (if there is one).
8. How does the melody differ in each of the sections? How do the chords progress and contrast between sections?

Your choice of Exercise:

EXERCISE #1:

Write your own song for one of the basic song structures.

1. Create whatever chord progressions you want in each section.
2. See if you can contrast each section by using different chord progressions and varying the melody.

EXERCISE #2:

Write your own song for one or more of the basic song structures.

1. You can also create lyrics that follow one of the song structures and partner with another student who will create the chords and the melody.
2. You can also create the lyrics and the melody and partner with someone on the chords.

Your choice of Exercise:

EXERCISE #1:

1. Analyze the form of two or three of your current favorite songs.
2. Write new lyrics to their melodies.
3. Write new melodies and chords for your lyrics.

EXERCISE #2:

1. Analyze the form of two or three of your current favorite songs.
2. Write new lyrics to their melodies.
3. Partner with another student who will create the chords and the melody.
4. You can also create the lyrics and the melody and partner with someone on the chords.

3
LYRICS

"Facts can be turned into art if one is artful enough."
—Paul Simon

"So what I do, more than play any instrument—I mean, I love to play—but more than that, I write songs. Songs that are about living, about what it's like to be going through all the things that people go through in life."
—Jackson Browne

WHAT IS A LYRIC?

A lyric tells a story, but it's not just a story. Unlike a story, a lyric doesn't stand by itself. Since it's not complete without the music, a lyric is only half of the picture.

Although a lyric can have poetic qualities, it's not really a poem either. The words of a lyric are joined to the music so we have to leave room for the music too. The words of the lyric also have to be singable.

Have you ever asked yourself any of these questions?

1. How do I communicate my thoughts and feelings with words and music?

2. How can I write the lyrics for my song in the most effective way possible?

3. How do I create words to move and inspire people?

4. How can I reach people so that they understand and even relate to what I'm trying to say?

> As songwriters, we want to make people care and to connect emotionally. Our story has to reach out and grab our listener. A great way to do this is to make it real and to make it true. The songs that we remember make us feel and experience something.

Here are three devices that can help people feel the truth in a lyric:

1. Use details and visual pictures. Details and images bring things alive and help the listener know exactly what and how we feel.

2. Involve human senses such as sight, sound, touch, taste, and smell to make the song real. This creates an experience more than just a story. Think about involving all of the senses.

3. Use more striking/original verbs and adjectives instead of ordinary ones. For example, you could choose between the words "cherish" or "treasure" instead of the more commonly used word "love."

LYRIC PLOT/STORY

Sometimes I think of songs as "pint-sized films" because they have to be able to tell a story in miniature form and in a very small amount of time. The lyric answers the questions "who, what, where, and when?"

You can actually plan your song out ahead of time! Here is a template that you may use, even before starting to write your lyric:

1. First verse: "In the first verse, I will describe and include..."

2. Second verse: "After the first verse, I will talk about..." "and then..." "and then, go to the..." (hint: Chorus!)

3. Chorus: Title; more generalized/universal/emotional—the theme of the song.

4. Last verse: "this will end like..." and/or "I will tie everything together with..." and go back to the...

5. Chorus: Title; the universal theme of the song—(again!)

> You can write down whatever comes into your head without judging or reworking it (sometimes called "automatic writing") to get your story on paper without worrying about rhymes or meter.

WHO (OR, POV, WHICH MEANS "POINT OF VIEW"):

Another strategy for writing compelling lyrics is to write from the first person as the point of view. Pretend to be the character in the song's story to create a more powerful, real experience for your listeners.

Pronouns tell us who's viewpoint it is. With POV, we have some choices:

1. First person (me, I, we): as in the song "Set Fire to the Rain" by Adele and Fraser T Smith; "Clocks" by Coldplay or "I Wanna Dance With Somebody" by George Merrill and Shannon Rubicam.

2. Second person (you): as in "You Light Up My Life" by Joe Brooks or "Light My Fire" by The Doors.

3. Third person (her, she, him, he, they, them, it): as in "She's in Love with the Boy" by Jon Ims or "She Loves You" by John Lennon/Paul McCartney of The Beatles.

The choice of POV will depend on each song. Experiment! ☺

Ask yourself which POV will make the stronger lyric. You can pretend you are that character (and maybe you are!) You can also pretend you are in the audience and hearing the lyric as if it were the first time.

Does the song keep your interest? Does the song move you? Can you relate? Sometimes when we change the point of view, we can make the lyric more powerful.

WHAT—VISUAL VERSUS EMOTIONAL:

1. When we write about what a person does or the inanimate things surrounding him or her, we create a reality and make pictures.

2. When we write about a person's emotional concerns, we are dealing with more philosophical, intellectual realms.

Songs with only feelings and thoughts can sometimes be a little uninteresting. But if we can build vivid images, emotions come alive and songs can be more engaging.

Putting more emphasis on images and details can help to connect us with the audience.

Breaking it down lyrically:

VERSE: contains the actions, objects, and descriptions.

CHORUS: contains the purpose, meaning, and emotions—the heart of the matter.

WHERE:

Where does the song take place? Try to get specific. Think visually so that the listener can really "see" this place. Use details, adjectives, and pictures!

WHEN:

When situations are vague, they're often less real and not as interesting. So, we can ask some questions to talk about things in terms of time:

1. When does the song's story take place?
2. Time of day?
3. Time of year?
4. Time of life?

EXERCISE:

VERBS AND ADJECTIVES

Take the following list of verbs and adjectives and find some imaginative replacements for each of them:

Run, Walk, Love, Listen, Cry, Talk, Hear, Try, Leave

Dark, Light, Faithful, Untrue, Happy, Sad, Beautiful, Alone, Soft

AUTOMATIC WRITING EXERCISE:

Set a timer for five minutes. Start writing as soon as your timer is set and just go for it! Write in paragraph form—don't worry about lyric phrases and/or rhymes. Describe a person, place, thing or time (in the past, right now, or someday) that made, make, or could one day make you happy, sad, mad, joyous, loving, fearful, or trusting.

Involve the senses to connect with a potential listener. Use imaginative verbs and adjectives. See if you can write with visual pictures and lots of details. When the timer goes off, you're done!

VISUAL AND EMOTIONAL EXERCISE, PART 1:

Think about whether the following lines contain more visual descriptions or emotions/thoughts/feelings, or combinations of both:

1. The chimney smoked
2. I'm lonely without you
3. A shadow fell across her face
4. I feel like you're gone for good
5. He's sorry that it's Monday again
6. She's walking on the frozen fields of winter
7. I grew up behind a white picket fence

VISUAL AND EMOTIONAL EXERCISE, PART 2:

Now, write three sentences/phrases with visual images and description and three that describe emotions/thoughts/feelings.

See if you can combine both of these elements in your songs.

RHYMES

Here are some examples of different kinds of rhymes:

1. Perfect Rhymes: the vowels and the final consonant sounds match precisely. (Examples: dog/hog, night/fight, sky/lie, white/kite)

Traditional thinking is to go for perfect rhymes only. In pop music, it's not always necessary. If you have a perfect rhyme but it changes the meaning of your song, you can go to another choice of rhyme.

Some lyricists (especially of show tunes) still use only perfect rhymes, but there are many songwriters now who don't always use them.

2. Imperfect Rhymes (aka "family rhymes," "false rhymes," or "slant rhymes"): the accented vowels are precise and the final consonant is *similarly* tied. It's almost a rhyme, but not quite (yet it works!) because they use words that give the feeling of rhyme but that aren't truly identical sounds. (Examples: lark/heart, lame/stain, pet/wreck, down/sound)

3. Open rhymes: there is no hard consonant at the end of the word. These kinds of words work well with held notes. (Examples: lie/buy, say/bay)

4. Closed rhymes: end with a consonant that stops our mouths. So, since we have to close our mouth at the end of the word, it often works well to use closed rhymes on notes that are not sustained or held out. (Examples: bed/head, lap/tap, park/lark, sat/hat)

5. Internal rhymes: the rhyme happens inside the lyric line, such as: "I know that we'll grow old together."

6. One syllable rhymes (masculine rhymes): such as "tree/bee," or it can be a multi-syllable rhyme, where the last syllable contains the rhyme. (Example: compare/despair)

7. Two syllable rhymes (feminine rhymes): the rhyme is in the syllable before the last. (Examples: lover/uncover or stalker/walker)

8. Three syllable rhymes (triple rhymes): where three syllables work together. (Examples: believing/receiving or institution/distribution)

When working with rhymes, we can strive to make the lines sound like ordinary speech—the way we sound when we are actually just talking to someone.

While I'm thinking of it, save yourself some time and energy—don't try to find a rhyme for "orange!" (If you do find one, please send me an email! ☺)

At the same time that we create our rhymes, we:

1. Tell our story (from the beginning, to the middle, to the end)

2. Provide the emotion

> Try to go for what you really want to say, not just the rhymes. This is the challenge!

POETIC DEVICES:

Poets use techniques called poetic devices, and lyricists can use them too!

1. Assonance: the emphasized vowels agree, but the final consonant sounds are dissimilar. (Examples: slip/hill, trail/grace, sleep/fleet)

2. Consonance: the vowel sounds are not alike, but the ending consonants are alike. (Examples: stack/lock, pit/pat, hog/sag, hip/hop! ☺)

3. Alliteration: when two or more consonants sound the same. (Examples: forever and for always, a winter's wind, one thousand thanks)

4. Similes: compare things with "like" or "as." (Examples: "as soft as snow," "her face was like a whispered dream")

5. Metaphors: observe or describe things without using "like" or "as." (Examples: "She was a wall," "I am a fallen tree")

EXERCISE:

Make up two of your own examples for each of the following:

Perfect rhyme

Imperfect rhyme

Assonance

Consonance

Alliteration

The trick is to create the rhyme and yet make it sound true. Try not to pick a word just because it rhymes. Strive for every day expressions (like real conversation!), and make your rhymes fit with the story.

If you think it sounds forced, you can rework the lyric and change the last word you're trying to rhyme.

EXERCISE: Can you think of some more imperfect rhymes? Now, see if you can turn some of them around and make them "perfect!"

FUN WITH ADDING EXTRA SPICE AND EXTRA INTEREST

An oxymoron is a figure of speech that combines contradictory terms. We can use creative plays on words by finding opposites and putting them together.

Examples of titles that do this are:

"I Got It Bad (and That Ain't Good)" by Duke Ellington and Paul Francis Webster

"Hurts So Good" by John Mellencamp

"The Sound of Silence" by Paul Simon

THREE EXERCISES:

1. Write a list of five to ten words and find their opposites.
2. Think of three examples of assonance for a lyric line (such as, "don't bait me with your game.")
3. Think of three examples of alliteration for a lyric line (such as, "how come my heart hurts?" or "now that he's near me")

RHYMING PATTERNS

We will frequently see patterns of rhymes in four-line lyrics where the rhymes appear at the ends of lines two and four. Another pattern is to have rhymes at the ends of lines one and two and then different rhymes for lines three and four.

HERE ARE SOME COMMON RHYME PATTERN POSSIBILITIES

Four-line sections:

1. rhyme two and four
2. rhyme one and three; two and four
3. rhyme one and two; three and four

Six-line sections:

1. rhyme one and two; four and five; three and six
2. rhyme one and two; three and four; five and six

See if you can experiment and come up with some more combinations!

Once you have created your rhyme scheme, use the same pattern throughout the rest of the verses. The choruses will have a different pattern and they will use their own (identical) pattern each time. If you write a bridge, you will use another pattern again.

Extra note:
Homophones are not rhymes. They are words that are spelled differently, but they sound the same. Homophones don't really work very well for lyrics.

Here are some examples: sale/sail, bye/buy, male/mail, rein/rain/reign, to/two/too.

REMEMBERING OUR TOOLS OF THE TRADE (from chapter 1):

These are such great devices to get your mind going and your juices flowing!

1. The Thesaurus: You can use this to come up with synonyms (words that mean the same thing) when you need them, and also, antonyms (opposites). I like *Roget's International Thesaurus of English Words and Phrases*. For online, I like: http://thesaurus.com/

2. A Rhyming Dictionary: I like to use *The Complete Rhyming Dictionary and Poet's Craft Book* by Clement Wood. For online, I like: http://www.rhymezone.com/

EXERCISE:

Write a four-line section of lyrics and put the rhyme schemes into two different orders.

Write a six-line section of lyrics and put the rhyme schemes into two different orders.

How are music and lyrics related?

1. A lyric has lines and music has phrases
2. A rhyme scheme goes with the length of the musical phrase
3. The music can suggest the placement of the rhyme.

The following are a few exercises that teach the subconscious mind to be on the lookout for new ideas. You will automatically be "programmed" to do it once you start. Keep your journal handy!

EXERCISE:

Everyday journal-writing exercise:

1. Set a timer for five or ten minutes or for whatever you decide to be the amount of time you think might work best for you. You might want to start with five minutes and see how it goes; see if you like doing it for longer and then, go to ten!
2. Free-associative writing or stream of consciousness: just write, write, write—whatever-comes-into-your-head-and-don't-look-back kind of writing! Just put it down; don't reread or judge it.
3. Do this everyday for five days to start out. Then, see if you can get into the habit of doing this everyday for a month—and then, from now on! Decide on a specific time to write each day and commit to that. If five days a week is too much at first, you can make it a certain day or two of the week at a certain time.
4. Fill a page or two, or however much you get done by the time the timer goes off.

This journal will be a gold mine of ideas for you. You will discover great lyric lines, titles, concepts, maybe even some rhymes! From these pages, you can pick and choose things that stand out as good or that suggest song possibilities.

Later on, if you're ever staring at a blank page and feeling lost or stumped for material, you can open your trusty journal and. . .who knows what brilliant song you can create from there!

EXERCISE:

1. Watch your favorite TV show (with your notebook or journal close at hand).
2. Listen for things that might inspire you to write "hooky" phrases or ideas or titles. This is all for possible use later on when you're songwriting.

I'm not suggesting that you take down exact bits of dialogue or conversation, as written and created by someone else. However, you can watch shows and get inspired by ideas and inspired by life.

This is an exercise to allow little "snippets" of conversations to stimulate you toward ideas that can get your own original creative juices flowing.

EXERCISE:

Note down snippets of conversations you happen to hear between people. You might be in a restaurant for example, and hear someone say something that grabs you! Or you might listen to some great dialogue between friends, family, and/or yourself—and jot that down!

Literary Factoid:

The great American writer, F. Scott Fitzgerald, was known for keeping little index cards of overheard conversations—which he then put to very wonderful use in his work.

EXERCISE:

Find inspiration for song ideas when you:

1. Listen to the news
2. Listen to a talk show
3. Go to a movie

EXERCISE:

Get inspired by the main character of one of your favorite books. You can ask yourself: How might someone like that feel? What could she/he think? Now write a song as if you were describing that kind of personality.

You can even pretend to *be* this kind of character. So, instead of thinking of "she/he," you are now telling the story first person to add power and make it even more real. Imagine that you are this type of individual and see how you might feel.

You can find ideas from *any* book you read where the character moves you in some way.

A character that draws you in and makes an impression on your heart and soul has the capacity to motivate you to create.

Get inspired by protagonists, interesting characters, heroes/heroines, villains, angels, and demons.

Here are some ideas for characters/stories/books you might want to get energized by:

1. Fern—*Charlotte's Web* by E.B. White
2. Henry—*Henry Huggins* (and other books about Henry Huggins) by Beverly Cleary
3. Holden—*Catcher In The Rye* by J.D. Salinger
4. Scout or Jem—*To Kill A Mockingbird* by Harper Lee
5. Mary Lennox or Colin—*The Secret Garden* by Frances Hodgson Burnett
6. Laura—*Little House In The Big Woods* (and others in this series) by Laura Ingalls Wilder
7. The Boy—*Sounder* by William H. Armstrong
8. Milo—*The Phantom Toll Booth* by Norton Juster
9. Laila or Miriam—*A Thousand Splendid Suns* by Khaled Hosseini
10. Charlie Bucket—*Charlie and the Chocolate Factory*—by Roald Dahl

More books and/or plays to read for inspiration:

1. *Holes* by Louis Sachar
2. *The Kite Runner* by Khaled Hosseini

3. *The Glass Menagerie* by Tennessee Williams

4. *A Streetcar Named Desire* by Tennessee Williams

5. *The Great Gatsby* by F. Scott Fitzgerald

6. *My Dog Skip* by Willie Morris

7. *Huckleberry Finn* by Mark Twain

8. *Tom Sawyer* by Mark Twain

9. *A Wrinkle In Time* by Madeleine L'Engle

10. *Old Yeller* by Fred Gipson

11. *The Haunting Of Hill House* by Shirley Jackson

12. *Half Magic* by Edward Eager

13. *Lord Of The Flies* by William Golding

14. *Nineteen Eighty-Four* by George Orwell

EXERCISE:

After you've written out some automatic writing on whatever subject you're writing about:

1. Take the *verse* of a favorite song.
2. Map out the exact number of syllables in each line of the verse you've chosen.
3. Write your own words to a new original verse with your subject matter, using the exact pattern of lines and syllables of the verse you chose to map out.
4. Take the *chorus* of a completely different song (another favorite maybe).
5. Map out the exact number of syllables in each line of the chorus you've chosen.
6. Write your own words to your chorus, using the exact pattern of lines and syllables of the chorus you chose to map out.
7. Improvise and play with a chord progression and melody to fit over a groove suggested by the "rhythm" of your new words. See how it all comes out! Refine and rewrite as needed.

LYRICS AND MUSICAL PHRASES

Lyric phrases go hand in hand with musical phrases. They have to belong together in order to work. This also means that the musical phrase will be as long as (or as short as) the lyrical phrase. They will match!

The last line in a segment can be a great place to put your main point, the thought that you want people to pay attention to. Often, that's the spot where the line stands out the most.

You can make your verse with little lines and your chorus with drawn-out lines (or vice versa) in order to create contrast from one section to the next.

LYRICS AND RHYTHM

Just as there is rhythm in music, there is a rhythmic element to lyrics. Let's think about the rhythm that is found in the syllables of words.

If we examine a dictionary, we can see all the words that are categorized there. We can also see that the words that contain two syllables and more than two syllables will have an accent over the more pronounced syllable.

This concept helps us musically! The melody will have notes that are higher, lower, shorter, longer, softer, or louder than others. Similarly, the syllables of words will have those kinds of stresses as well.

We can keep all this in mind when putting words and music together so that the beats, stresses, and rhythms of the music go hand in hand with the beats, stresses, and rhythms of the lyrics.

How do we match the rhythm with the words?

1. Make sure that the words fit easily with the music and that the accents are on the right syllables.
2. There are often many rhythmic ways to set a lyric line. You can experiment using various rhythms for your lyrics and their syllables and decide what works best.

Let's take an example and use a simple line: "I lose myself to you." In 4/4, this could be set a number of different ways, and that may change the meaning of the song.

Different Rhythmic Ways To Set A Lyric

Lisa Donovan Lukas

There are often many ways to set a lyric line, depending what you want to say and what you want to emphasize. See how the different rhythmic musical choices emphasize different words in each example. The first example emphasizes LOSE and YOU, the second example emphasizes MY-SELF and the third example emphasizes I. When we emphasize different words rhythmically, we have the ability to change the meaning.

LYRICS, MUSIC, AND PROSODY

Prosody is when the feeling of the lyric and the music go together. For example, we don't usually use a chipper/happy little melody for a dark, sad lyric. A minor key might convey sadness better...you get the picture! (It might not though, so be sure to experiment! ☺)

How do we make sure that lyrics and music go together?

1. Find out if the words will sing effortlessly by singing them yourself as you work out your song.
2. Be certain the tempo is right for the amount of words you've got going on. Sometimes when you speed up the tempo, a lyric can suddenly become too wordy!
3. Also, keep major versus minor keys in mind, in terms of the feelings you want to convey.

EXERCISE:

Write a hypothetical few lines of lyric and see how many different ways you can set the lyric, both rhythmically and melodically.

Sing them and listen to how the melodies will change to go with different rhythmic choices and different accents of your lyric syllables. Some will fit more naturally than others. Experiment! You can do this first with lyric to melody and then, melody to lyric, either way. Emphasize different words and different syllables and see what happens!

UNIQUENESS

Try to avoid "clichés": for example, "You are my dream come true," "You broke my heart," and "I need you," or "I love you." Here's another one: "Oh baby." You get the idea. ☺

You might also want to stay away from cliché rhymes, such as:

1. Moon/june
2. Miss/kiss
3. Dance/chance
4. Love/above

See if you can stretch yourself and find original and unique twists on things.

PLANNING YOUR STORY

Zero in on a condensed version of what you want to say. See if you can describe your song's emotion in a concise way. Write down in one sentence what your song is about.

EXERCISE:

Take three songs you love:

1. See if you can express the feeling or emotion each song conveys in just a few words.
2. Write a very brief synopsis for each song.

TITLES IN THE LYRIC

We all remember titles that hold our attention and engage us.

When a title is interesting and catches our attention, we want to find out more. We want to hear that song!

Creating catchy titles:

1. Construct titles out of ordinary expressions, words, or figures of speech.
   For example: "Odds and Ends" (Bacharach/David), "Yesterday" (Lennon/McCartney), "Let It Be" (Lennon/McCartney), or "Every Breath You Take" (Sting)

2. Invent titles from ordinary phrases that you then twist around or combine with opposites:
   For example: "A Hard Day's Night" (Lennon/McCartney), "You're Nobody 'Til Somebody Loves You" (Morgon/Stock/

Cavanaugh), "Killing Me Softly with His Song" (Fox/Gimbel), or "Eight Days a Week" (Lennon/McCartney)

EXERCISE:

Brainstorm and see if you can come up with three titles that use everyday, ordinary expressions.

Then, see if you can come up with three titles that are a "play on words"—use opposites or twists on things to see what you can come up with!

EXERCISE:

Keep your notebook/journal with you. When a concept or title comes to you, write it down. Return to that idea during your writing time. If you note these ideas down as they come to you, you won't forget them, and you will have them "at the ready" to work on later.

EXERCISE:

Create a song by answering the questions "who, what, where, and when?" Plan your song out ahead of time with the following template that you can use, even before starting to write your lyric.

Write a few paragraphs first that describe the story/plot of your song. Then complete these sections:

1. First verse: "In the first verse, I will describe and include..."
2. Second verse: "After the first verse, I will talk about..." and "then, it will lead to..."
3. Chorus: Title; more generalized/universal/emotional.
4. Last verse: "This will end like..." and/or "I will tie everything together with...and lead back to the..."
5. Chorus: Title; the universal theme of the song—(again!)

4
MELODY

"As long as I can say what it is that I need to say, then I'll fit whatever I'm trying to say around a melody."
—Alanis Morissette

"I love being a very personal singer/songwriter, but I also like being a scientist or explorer."
—Bjork

STEPS, INTERVALS, AND PHRASES IN MELODY

What is an interval?

An interval is the distance between two pitches.

What is a step?

In Western music the smallest interval from one note to the next closest note, lower or higher, is called a half step, or a minor 2nd. Notes that are two half steps lower or higher from each other are whole steps, or Major 2nds.

We can construct melody with a collection of approaches such as:

1. Using intervals of steps
2. Big interval jumps
3. ...and little interval jumps
4. Repeating musical ideas to help our listeners remember and, hopefully, want to sing along with our song
5. Short-and-sweet concepts. In other words, they are catchy!
6. Sometimes, we can even make up a nice melodic phrase with just two or three notes! BTW: Have you ever heard "One Note Samba" by Antonio Carlos Jobim? It's such a great song! (Music and English lyrics by Jobim; Portuguese lyrics by Newton Mendoça)

We want our melody to be catchy, enduring, and singable, and we also want it to hold our attention; to be enjoyable, and maybe even surprising.

Here's the thing: we want to keep our ears interested!

For our melodies, we have the use of:

1. half steps (minor seconds)
2. whole steps (major seconds)
3. skips (a third or more)

Why choose one note over another? A lot can depend on your mood at the time as well as the feelings you want to express.

MELODY AND INTERVALS

The distance between any note and another note is called an interval. The number of half steps between the intervals of a scale will be the same in any key.

When you play notes separately, one after another, you are playing a melody. The distance between each of these notes is called a melodic interval. When you play them at the same time, they are harmonic intervals.

Take a look at the examples of melodic and harmonic intervals on the next two pages (using middle C as our jumping off point).

Melodic Intervals

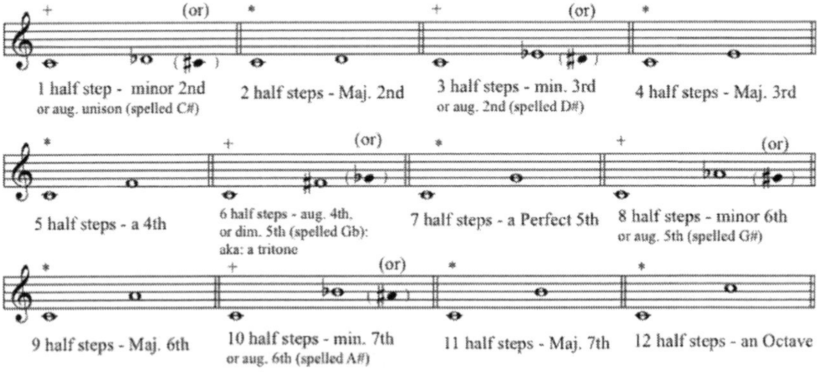

The distance between notes is called an interval. When you play notes separately, one after another, you are playing a melody. The distance between these notes is called a melodic interval.

The * sign is to designate intervals within the Major scale. These are called diatonic intervals. The + sign designates intervals outside of the (diatonic) Major scale and we call these chromatic intervals.

The notes in parentheses are different note spellings for the same note. These are called "enharmonics." Different spellings are sometimes used and are dependent upon what is going on musically.

Harmonic Intervals

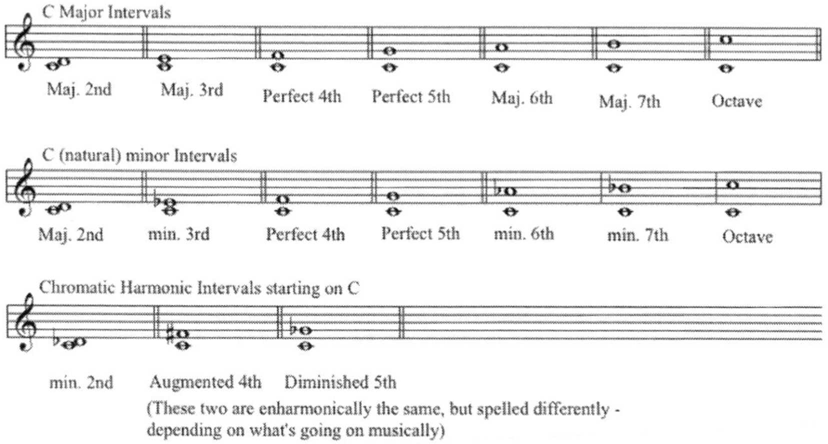

When you play the notes of an interval at the same time, they are called harmonic intervals. Here are examples of harmonic intervals in C major and C minor.

There are many kinds of scales and modes that we can use for our melodies—and we'll get to some of them in this book.

We can calculate the distance between the notes in whatever scale we decide to use. We can then create these same specific scales or modes using our calculations and starting on any note. This theory remains the same between all the different types of scales.

Mathematical Factoid:

The relationship between the different notes of the same types of scales in terms of the distance between the notes will be the same in every key.

For an example of this theory, let's use the key of C major. The distance between C and E is a major third (four half steps). Just as in the key of D major, the distance between D and F♯ is a major third (four half steps)—and so on, in every key. So the number of half steps between the notes of the C scale and the notes of the D scale are the same. All the intervals between these notes will be identical and the same principal will apply in any key.

Since the relationships in terms of distances between the notes of a certain scale are uniform in any key, you can therefore compute mathematically, the scale you want to use.

You can start on any note and count the correct distances between notes to figure out your scale. Your subsequent melody can be created from there. You can do this for any key you want to use.

Each diatonic major scale will have a relative minor scale. You can figure out what the relative minor scale is by counting down from your scale's starting point by three half steps. For example, with C, we would count down three half steps and land on A. So, A is therefore, the relative minor of C. The key signatures for both C and A minor will be the same.

If you count three half steps down from F, you will land on D. D is the relative minor of F major and they both share the same key signature, and so on.

EXERCISE:

Try experimenting to see if using a minor scale will make a melody sound more on the "sad" side, as opposed to the use of a more "happy" major scale. Did the use of a different scale change the emotion at all?

In addition to the Major scale and the relative natural minor, we have:

1. The melodic minor

2. The harmonic minor

3. Different modes

Let's take a look at examples of these scales and modes. Here are some common scales and modes. Their formulas in terms of whole and half steps (major and minor seconds) are shown in the first two scale examples. You can practice calculating the intervals in some of the other scales and modes.

Major, Minor Scales, Modes & Blues

(In these cases, we'll be looking at C as our starting point)

The Major Scale - (so, C major): **

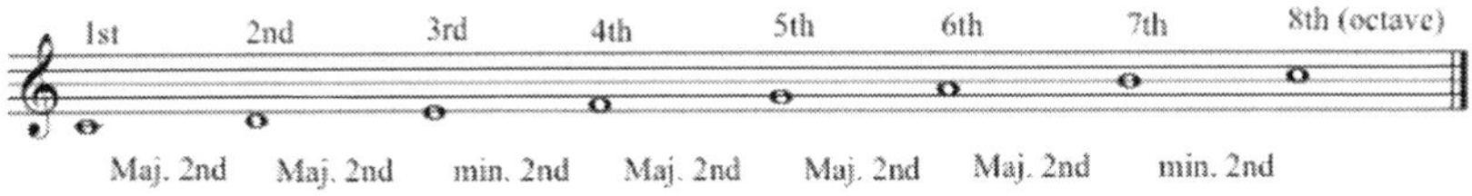

The Relative Natural Minor

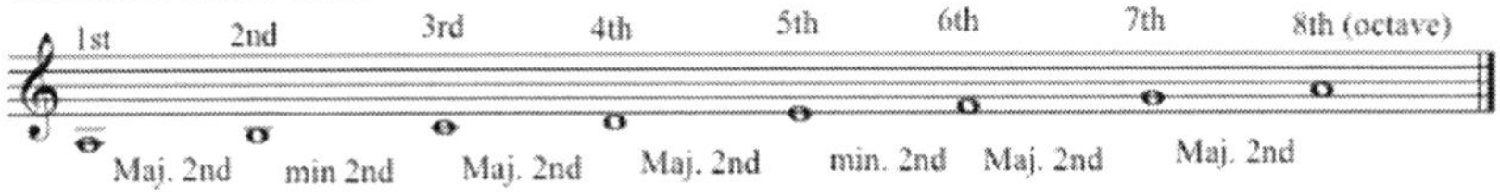

The melodic minor - has maj. 6th and maj. 7th (leading note) going up; a min. 7th and min. 6th going down)

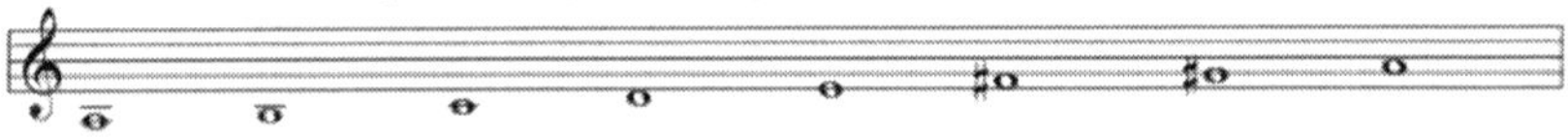

The harmonic minor - has min. 6th and the leading note (maj. 7th) going both up and down.

Dorian mode (the dorian mode has the same key signature as the major key a Maj. 2nd below the starting note of the dorian scale. For example C dorian shares the same key signature as Bb Maj. (two flats - Bb, Eb)

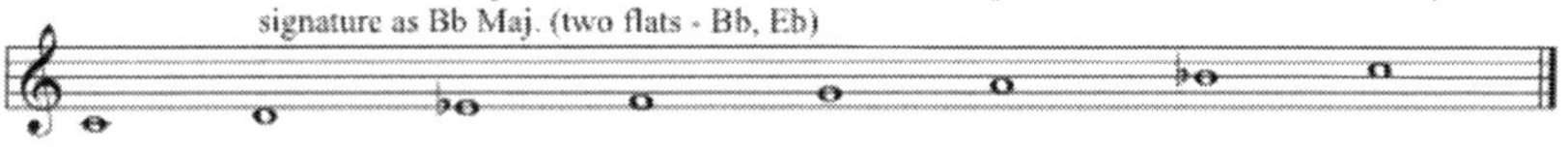

** you can count the intervals in all of these scales in the same way that I have illustrated in the first two scales.

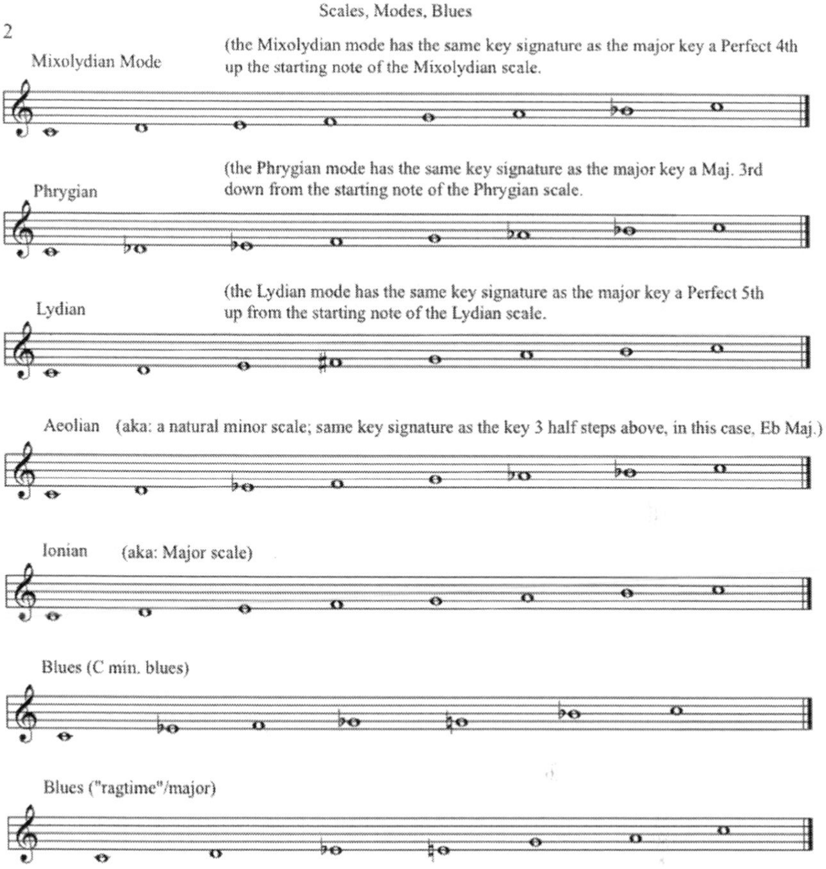

A scale can begin on any one of the twelve notes that are available. The key signature is the notation that tells us which notes are raised up (sharped) or dropped down (flatted) in order to let us know what key we're in for a particular music composition or song.

In musical notation, the key signature is the series of sharps or flats that are written immediately following the clef sign.

The key signature indicates to us what key we're in.

This defines our tonal center, the basic scale formula and harmonic context within a piece of music.

The choice of key is something to keep in mind when thinking about your singer and his or her vocal range.

Your choice of scale also affects the feel of your song as well as the message you want to express.

There are many kinds of scales at our disposal for our creativity in coming up with different melodic ideas.

EXERCISE:

Pick three different notes and a specific scale or mode.

Mathematically construct the scale or mode starting on each different note choice by analyzing your intervals/steps.

CONTRAST IN MELODY

We can employ contrasting ideas so that the different sections of the song stand out from each other. For example, the verse melody will contrast with the chorus melody.

With larger classical pieces, there is much more expansion and furtherance of ideas involved in the writing process. Still, it's interesting to know that repeated melodies (or ideas) and contrast (or variations) are used in creating both pop and classical music.

MELODIC RANGE

When we write pop melodies, we want to keep the singer's vocal range in mind.

> The characteristic range for a popular song generally falls into approximately one octave and a third—(give or take)!

We want to create melodies that are interesting and challenging, but not with gigantic ranges. We don't want our song to be so difficult that the artist is not able to hit the notes.

> Pop songs are not usually for singers with the vocal range of Renée Fleming!

Of course, pop music has always had incredible singers like Christina Aguilera, Whitney Houston, Michael Bolton, Celine Dion, Barbra

Streisand, and Mariah Carey. These are singers with amazing vocal ranges and ability.

Even so, we want to keep our melodic ranges in mind when we write. We want the singers to be comfortable singing the notes.

Vocal Ranges

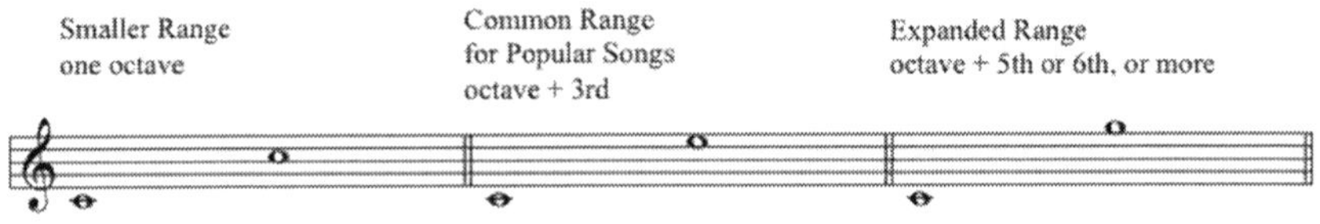

MELODY AND LYRIC

How do we create verses and choruses that we can repeat easily?

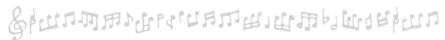

1. Each line in each lyric section has the exact same number of syllables, so that...

2. ...the corresponding melody will be the same for each section as well.

EXERCISE:

1. Study two or three of your favorite songs. See where the use of repetition occurs.
2. Take a couple patterns of repetition, and use that as a template for your own lyric and melody.
3. Create your syllables and rhythm in the same pattern using your own words and your own melody.

WRITING MELODIES

Composing a melody isn't really just about playing some chord patterns and seeing what happens next as we sing (or improvise) along. We can get started that way, but ultimately, we want to craft melodies that aren't completely dependent upon our chord progressions.

We want our melody to stand by itself. Also, we want our melody to be singable, easy for others to sing along with—and memorable too.

The melody and the lyric should go together. We want to make sure the feeling of the melody matches the feeling of the lyric.

MELODY AND THE TITLE

The part of the song that contains the title needs to stand out melodically from the other parts of the melody. Here are a couple of ways we can do this:

1. Change the rhythm up!
2. Change the range.

MELODY AND PHRASES

1. First off, we can begin with a new concept or a snippet of something we like.
2. Invent a short memorable (something catchy!) idea. In music, this idea is called a "motive."
3. Develop one or two measures into longer lines by repeating or varying them (or a combo of both).
4. Enlarge these musical ideas into the sections of the song.

We can also use two melodic ideas (often known as "call-and-response," which is like a "question/answer" or an "echo" effect) and take turns by using first one, then the other, so that things don't get too monotonous.

We can use a variation of the first idea (aka: the "motive") and then repeat it (1 to 1-a, and 1 to 1-a again), or we can use two completely different ideas/motives (1 to 2, and 1 to 2 again).

Melody and Phrases

Beginning ideas/motives

Lisa Donovan Lukas

Example 1

Example 2

We can use two melodic ideas (aka: "call and response" or "question/answer") and take turns by using the first one, then the other.

We can either use a variation of the first idea (called a "motive") and then repeat it (1 to 1- a; 1 to 1- a again) or create two completely different motives (1 to 2, and 1 to 2 again.)

Expanding Melodic Phrases

Lisa Donovan Lukas

When you have written an eight bar section using variation and repetition, you can then work on expanding it into a finished song with the use of contrast.

The methods we use to "grow" or develop the music in our songs are:

1. Variation 2. Repetition 3. Contrast

> When you have written an eight bar section using variation and repetition, you can then work on extending it into a finished song with the use of contrast.

Different sections can be created from the first section with the use of some of these approaches:

1. Alter the quality of your rhythms. For example, you can use more complex rhythms in one section and simpler, less complicated rhythms in another.

2. Switch up the duration of your melodic lines. For example, if your verse has concise lines, write elongated lines for the chorus (or the other way around).

3. Go higher or lower with the range of the vocal.

> Melody writing is the art of using methods of variation, repetition, and contrast.

We can:

1. Change a motive (use two different motives)

2. Copy a motive (use the identical motive twice)

3. Embellish and enlarge upon a motive

4. Build our ideas into differing sections

Expanding Melodic Phrases
& Contrasting Sections

Lisa Donovan Lukas

Here is an example of expanding melodic motives as well as the creation of a contrasting section. The B section goes higher in range than the A section and uses more rhythmic syncopation.

The A section is expanded the first time by repeating it twice (with slight variations in bars 8 and 16) and is stated only once at the return, after the B section.

All this time, we keep our vocalist in mind. We utilize the choice of scale, depending upon the emotion and the subject matter we want to convey in our song.

We can experiment with combinations of steps and skips to create our melodies. We can build our vocal lines in this way, inside the confines of our scale.

EXERCISE:

1. Write a musical phrase by using the "call-and-response" idea: take turns by alternating between the first short motive and then the second, so that things don't get too repetitive or predictable.
2. You can either alternate by using a variation of the first idea and then repeating (1 to 1-a, and 1 to 1-a again) or you can use two completely different ideas (1 to 2, and 1 to 2 again). Make this phrase four bars long.
3. Now, repeat your four-bar phrase and expand your song. You might want to slightly alter the second repeat (of the four bars) to make things more interesting or surprising. See what you come up with. Now you will have eight bars for your first section. (A)
4. Create a contrasting B section with a brand new motive/idea. If your first A section had short rhythmic lines, use longer lines and rhythms for your B section—or vice versa. If your A section was lower in range, make the melody in your B section go higher—or vice versa. (*More advanced: Think about making the last bar (or last two bars) of your B section end on the V chord. That is to say, whatever note(s) you choose for these bars will work with the V chord. This will help lead you back to your A section very easily.)
5. Now go back and repeat the first eight bars of your A section to finish.
6. Ta dah!! You now have expanded melodic phrases and a contrasting section under your belt (A, B, A). Good work!

(* note for # 4 in the preceding Exercise: Chords and Roman numerals will be covered in more detail in the next chapter on harmony. Feel free to come back and experiment with this later!)

5
HARMONY

"These are the sort of things that push you on in music—the curiosity, a passion for new ideas."
—Elvis Costello

"[But] it's important that you visit your worksite every day, even if it's just to improvise, touch the piano, play some chords. Be in touch with your music."
—Burt Bacharach

The study of theory and harmony is deep. We can find volumes of books (and then some!) on these subjects. The extensive study of theory and harmony reaches far beyond what I will cover in this book on songwriting. But if harmony/theory is the ocean, we're still going to get our feet wet and start to swim! Meanwhile, if you've been playing an instrument for a while, you have also already been studying harmony and theory in your music lessons and classes.

On the other hand, if you're just beginning to learn an instrument, you will find that the study of theory and harmony will be an on going part of your process.

If you're a brand new beginner and haven't studied any theory or harmony at all yet, you can take a look at some of these ideas and use them as jumping-off points to get started. Be patient, experiment, and enjoy each step.

Question: How can I get started with some of these harmonic ideas?

1. Look through the harmony examples in this chapter to check out some of the rudimentary ideas, even if it all seems completely new to you at first.

2. Let these principals inspire the idea that there is a connection between the understanding of harmony and theory and the way that they are tied to songwriting.

3. Think about the way that harmony, theory, and composition can free you to create the kinds of songs you want to write.

4. Allow these thoughts and ideas to set you off in some new creative directions.

5. Experiment, tinker, fiddle around. See what happens.

KEY

The key of a piece is a set of notes that are drawn toward one note, which we call the tonic. The tonic note is the center and assigns the name of the key. For example, C is the tonic in the key of C major and C minor.

When we think about major and minor tonality, the key of a piece determines the scale we use. There are many kinds of scales and modes. Here are some examples of popular scales for songs, as well as some examples of songs you can listen to for each of the corresponding scales:

1. The major scale (as used in "A Groovy Kind Of Love" by Toni Wine and Carole Bayer Sager and "I Wanna Dance With Somebody" by George Merrill and Shannon Rubicam)

BTW: I heard that "A Groovy Kind of Love" was apparently inspired by the Rondo movement of Muzio Clementi's Sonatina in G major, op. 36 no. 5! Take a listen. . .what do you think?

2. The minor scale (as used in "Livin' La Vida Loca" by Desmond Child and Draco Rosa and "Set Fire to the Rain" by Adele Adkins and Fraser Thorneycroft-Smith)

3. The dorian mode (as used in "Oye Como Va" by Tito Puente, "Moondance" by Van Morrison, and "Scarborough Fair" (English Folk Song with a very well-known version by Simon and Garfunkel)

4. The mixolydian mode (as used in "You Learn" by Alanis Morissette and Glen Ballard, and "Paperback Writer" by John Lennon and Paul McCartney)

5. The blues scale (as used in "After Midnight" by J.J. Cale, "Heartbreaker" by Jimmy Page, Robert Plant, John Paul Jones, and John Bonham, "Pink Cadillac" by Bruce Springsteen, and "Sunshine of Your Love" by Jack Bruce, Pete Brown, and Eric Clapton)—Check out both major and minor blues scales at the end of this chapter if you would like to experiment with their different tones.

INTERVALS

An interval is the distance between two notes. For example, if we count from C to D (1, 2) we have a 2nd. If we count from C to E (1, 2, 3), we have a 3rd. (You can take a look at the interval chart in my chapter on melody to review.)
An interval can be:

Perfect
Major
Minor
Augmented
Diminished

We can use the notes in the Major and minor scales to create intervals. To describe intervals, we use the numbers of the notes in the scale, and we also use the names. For instance, when we can say a Major 3rd or a minor 3rd, we are using a name as well as a number in both cases.

Intervals of seconds, thirds, sixths, and sevenths can be major or minor depending on the number of half steps we can count between them. For instance a minor 3rd involves three half steps and a Major 3rd is four half steps.

We call a group of intervals "perfect," and that includes the unison, 4th, 5th, and octave. They are consonant (aka: blending/harmonious), and when inverted, the interval that is created is also perfect. In the diatonic scale, all 4ths and 5ths are perfect. To "invert" for example, if we go from C up to F that's a Perfect 4th, and if we *invert* that and go from C down to F, that's a Perfect 5th.

An interval can be augmented if it is raised by half a step. Conversely, an interval can be diminished if it is lowered a half a step.

You will also find information about intervals in my chapter on melody, but, since they figure into the construction of chords as well, I wanted to touch upon them in both chapters.

What is an interval?

An interval is the distance between two notes.

You can experiment by playing and listening to the different intervals.

PRIMARY CHORDS

Let's use the C major scale to learn about primary chords. To begin, we see that there are seven notes in the scale. Since the major scale has seven notes, we can construct seven chords from those notes.

When we put numbers under each of the seven keys of the scale, we can see that the C chord is constructed on the 1st note of the scale. The F chord is constructed on the 4th note of the scale, and the G is on the 5th note of the scale. That's why we call these chords the one, four, five chords—and we usually see Roman numerals (like this: I, IV, and V) for the chords. These are our primary chords.

We create a triad (a chord with three notes, stacked in 3rds) on the first note of the scale. To do this we count 1 – 3 – 5, where 1 is the first note, 3 is the second note, and 5 is the third note. We call 1 the root note, we call

3 the third of the chord, and 5 is called the fifth of the chord. (These are intervals!) In this example, we would have C–E–G.

We create a triad on the fourth note of the scale (F) and come up with F–A–C. The fifth note (G) gives us G–B–D.

Primary chords are based on the perfect intervals of I to IV and I to V:

1. I (the *tonic* or C in this example)

2. IV (the *subdominant* or F in this example)

3. V (the *dominant* or G in this example).

> Primary chords are built on the:
> 1st note of any scale
> 4th note of any scale
> 5th note of any scale

Now we know that C, F, and G are the primary chords in the key of C major. The primary chords are the most frequently used chords in songs and you will see combinations of these progressions in songs many times. You will hear these chords over and over (and over!) again in blues, rock, folk, and pop songs. And because they are strong progressions, they work!

Of these three chords, the I chord (C in the key of C) is the strongest. It is called the tonic and is often referred to as coming "home." The V chord (G) is the chord that will cause tension and make us feel like we want to return back "home" to the I chord. The IV (F) chord will also return to the I chord or move to the V chord.

Harmonizing the C Major Scale

C Major Scale

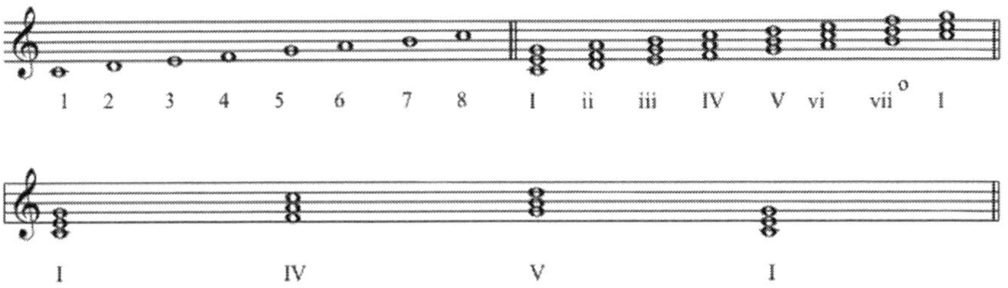

PRIMARY CHORDS: I IV V I

SECONDARY CHORDS: ii iii vi

THE CHORDS THAT ARE NOT PRIMARY ARE THE "AWAY" CHORDS. THEY DON'T GIVE US A REST OR PAUSE -- THEY DON'T GIVE US ANY KIND OF CADENCE. THEY ARE TRAVELLING AWAY FROM HOME.

Harmony involves the choice of chords for our songs. We get to pick the chords we want to use. We also get to decide when they happen. We can construct chords with the notes in our scale (diatonically), or we can create them using some of the notes that are not within our scale (chromatically). (These are called "altered" chords.)

The Roman numerals show us which scale-tone the chord is built on. They also show us whether the chord is major or minor and whether a 9th or an 11th has been added, etc. Capitals are used for major and lower case is for minor. The tiny symbol "o" is used for diminished chords.

Things definitely get more complicated from here! Even so, we can begin with these basic concepts. Allow yourself to experiment. Grab some chords and get started. See what comes up for you!

What are some popular chord progressions?

There are lots of common popular chord progressions available to us. Feel free to vary these progressions. Mix them up! Make up your own! Some progressions are seen (heard!) over and over again in popular songs, so I want to include them for you here.

POPULAR CHORD PROGRESSIONS

Major Key:

1. I – IV (for example, in the key of C: C – F)
2. I – IV – V (for example: C – F – G)
3. I – vi – IV – V (for example: C – Am – F – G)
4. I – vi – ii – V (for example: C – Am – Dm – G)
5. I – V/3 (1st inversion)—vi – I/5 (2nd inversion) – IV – I/3 – ii – V (for example: C – G/B – Am – C/G – F – C/E – Dm – G
6. I – ii – iii – IV (for example: C – Dm – Em – F)

Minor Key:

1. i – ♭VII (for example: Cm – B♭)
2. i – ♭VII – ♭VI – V (for example: Cm – B♭ – A♭ – G)

3. i – ♭VII – ♭VI – ♭VII (for example: Cm – B♭ – A♭ – B♭)

4. i – iv (Cm – Fm) or i – v (Cm – Gm)

Dorian Mode:

1. i – ii – ♭III – ii (for example: Cm – Dm – E♭ – Dm)

2. i – IV (for example: Cm – F)

Mixolydian Mode:

1. I – ♭VII – IV (for example: C – B♭ – F)

2. I – ♭VII (for example: C – B♭)

Popular "Twelve-Bar Blues" progression—(twelve measures, with chords in this order):

I (four bars)
IV (two bars) – I (two bars)
V (one bar) – IV (one bar) – I (two bars)—(variation: sometimes the last two bars are I [one bar] to V [one bar], instead of two bars of I)

For Example (in the key of C, using Dominant 7th chords):
C7 (four bars)
F7 (two bars) – C7 (two bars)
G7 (one bar) – F7 (one bar) – C7 (one bar) – G7 (one bar)
(You can take a look at the twelve-bar blues example on page one hundred eleven for a visual!)

HARMONIC STRUCTURE

To create form and structure harmonically, we can combine some popular chord progressions and construct the standard sections of a song. The use of different harmonic progressions for the separate sections of a song helps to keep things fresh and differentiate between them.

Here is an example for the structure of ABAB (Verse/Chorus/Verse/Chorus).
If we want eight bars for each section, we'll combine a couple of typical progressions and see what we come up with for our different sections:

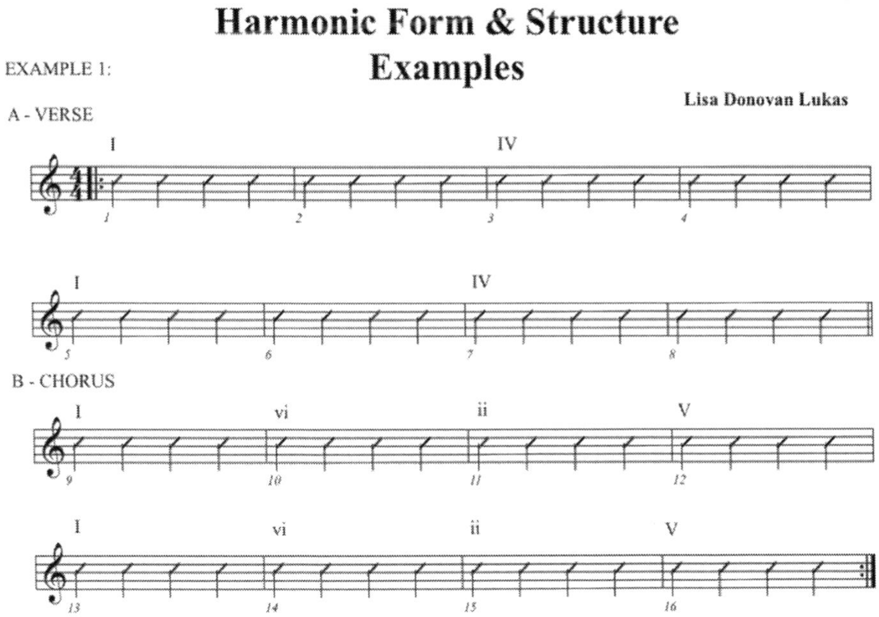

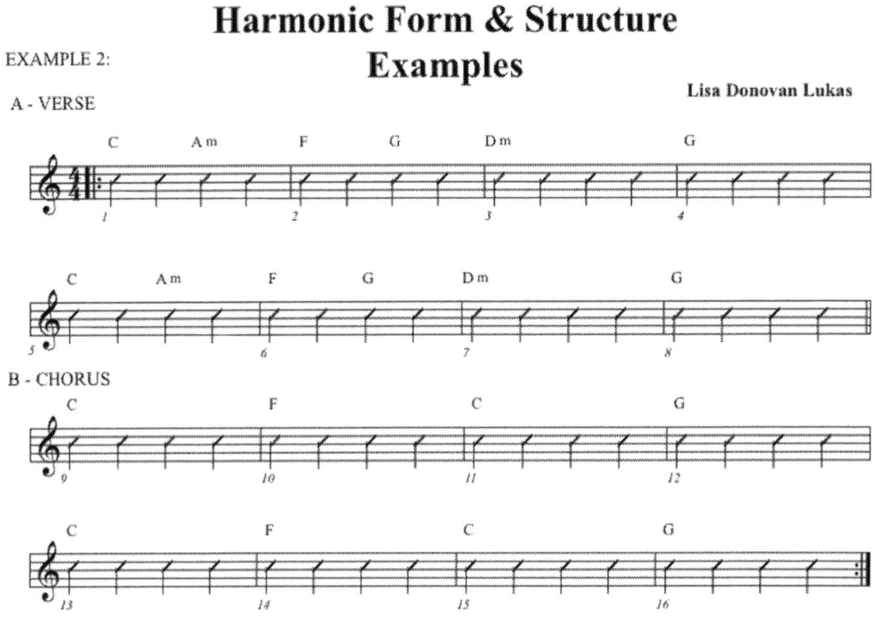

> EXERCISE:
>
> Build your own verse and chorus by selecting two common progressions and putting them together in a way that pleases you.

> EXERCISE:
>
> Select two of your favorite songs and pick the chord progressions from one of the song's verses and the other song's chorus. Combine the two progressions to create your own verse and chorus. Then write your own melody and lyrics to go with it.

COMMON HARMONIC STRUCTURES FROM BACK IN THE DAY

1. In the 1950's, loads of popular songs used the I, IV, V, I progression as well as the I, vi, IV, V, I progression (and it's variation: I, vi, ii, V, I).

2. There was also the use of the twelve-bar blues progression (in rock 'n roll!): I, I, I, I (four bars), IV, IV (two bars), I, I (two bars), V (one bar), IV (one bar), I, I (two bars).

12 Bar Blues Example

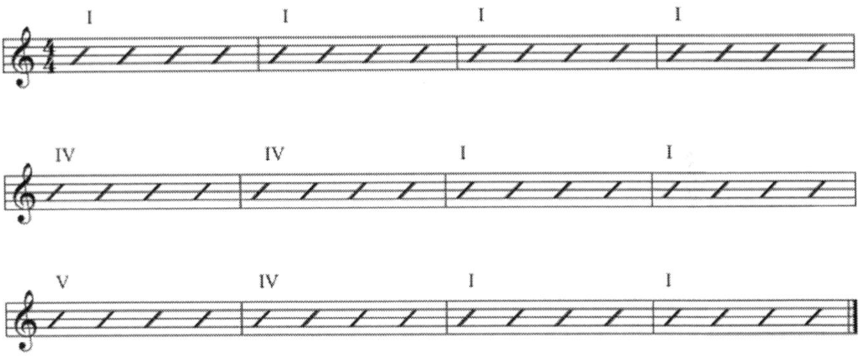

When we hear these chord patterns, we feel we already know them (because we've heard them so many times!), so we know what to expect. And since we're so accustomed to them, we remember them.

When creating our songs, we can use these basic ideas in imaginative ways to maintain interest and originality. With a little inventiveness, we can allow these classic structures to help us make something new and exciting with our own material. Different songs may have the same kinds of progressions, but the melodies and the lyrics will be unique.

IDEAS FOR VARIATION AND CONTRAST

1. Expand or contract a progression (e.g., C – F – C – F or I – IV – I – IV)

2. Alter the sequence of the chords

3. Alter the rhythmic placement of the chords in the chord progression.

Ideas for Variation & Contrast with Chord Progressions

Lisa Donovan Lukas

1. Expand or contract a progression - C F C F (I - IV - I - IV) can be:

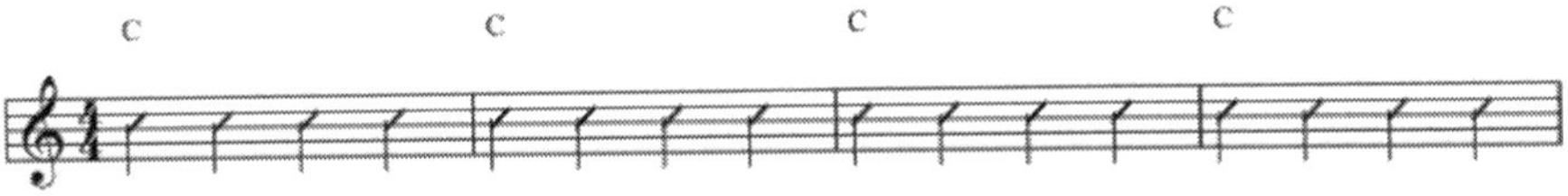

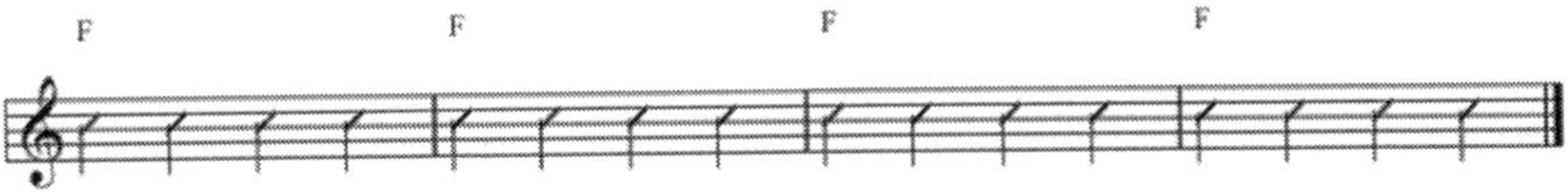

OR:

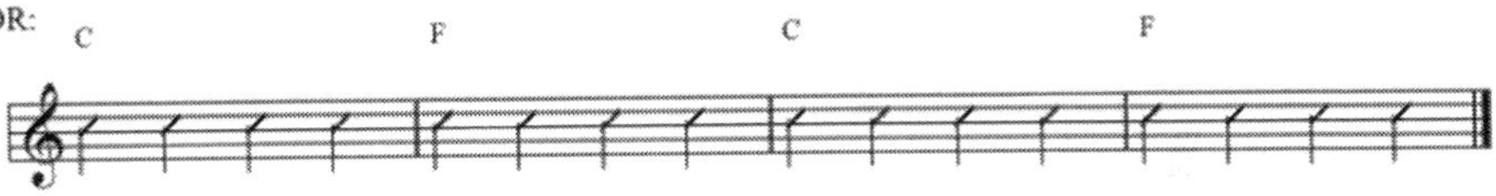

OR:

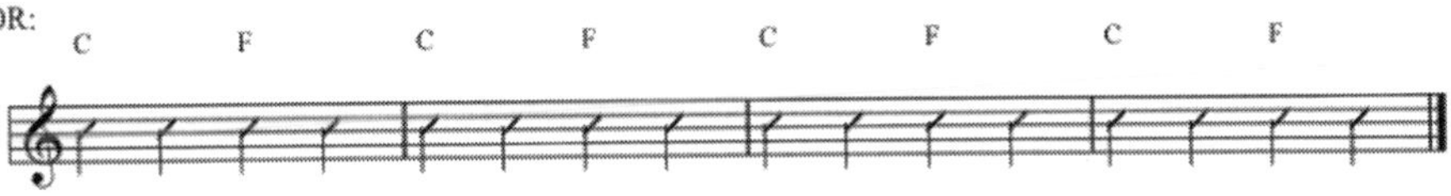

OR:

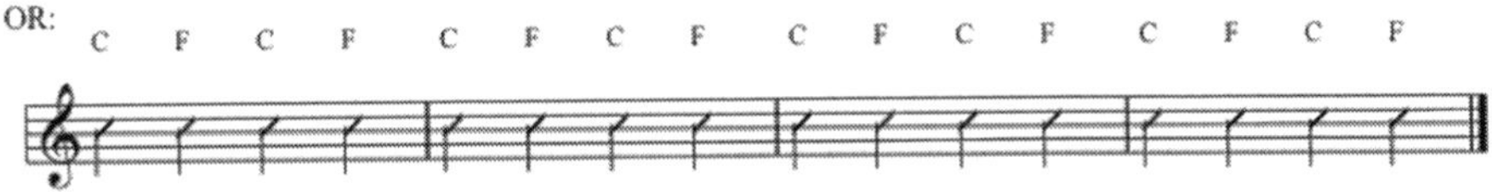

2. Alter the order of the chords:

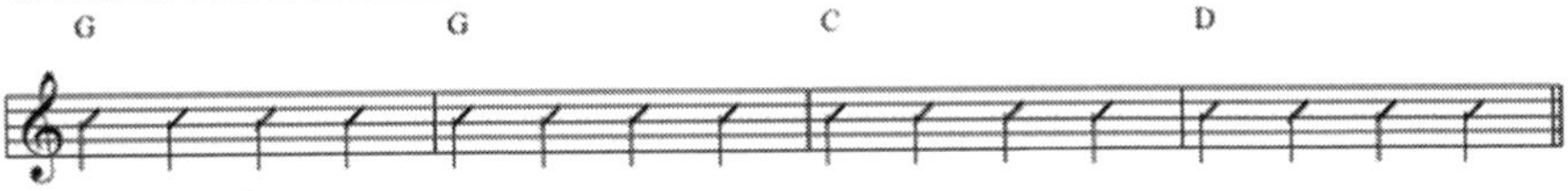

Could be altered to:

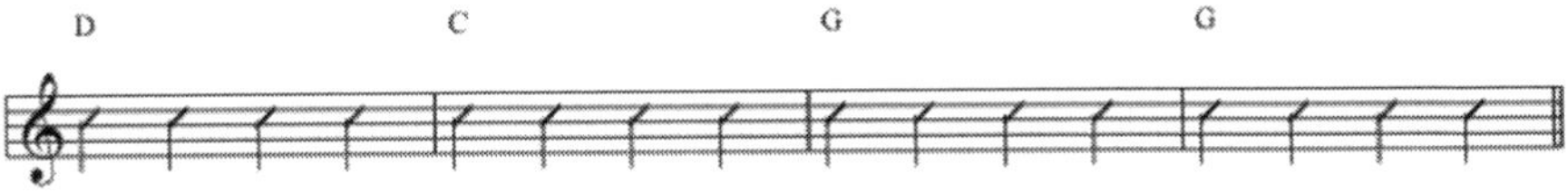

Variation and Contrast With Chord Progressions

2

3. Chord Placement - (alter the rhythmic placement of the chord progression):

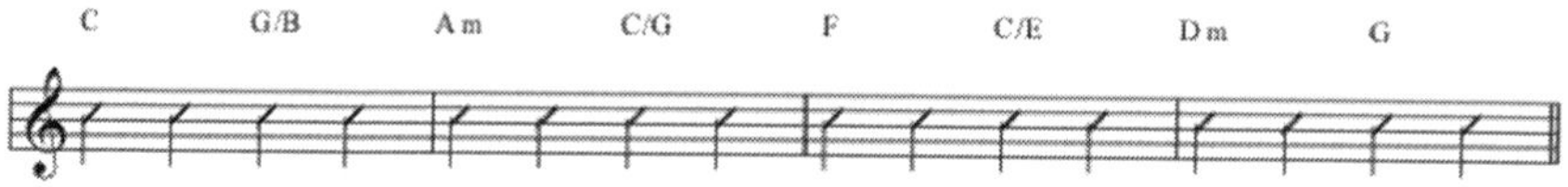

Could be altered to:

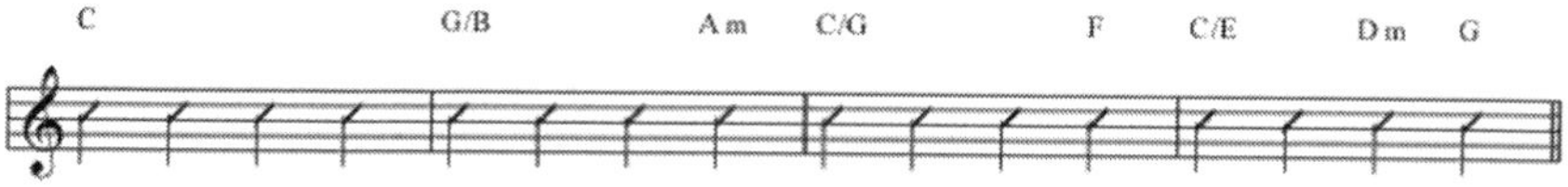

EXERCISE #1

Write a chord progression for your verse. Then write a contrasting chorus section. Write the melody and lyrics to go with these sections.

Here are your parameters for this exercise:

1. Use one chord per bar in your *verse*
2. Use two chords per bar in your *chorus*
3. Contrast your chord's rhythms (use different rhythmic duration for the chords)
4. Use contrasting chord progressions for each section

EXERCISE #2

Try another version of the above exercise using some more colorful chords. Take a look at page one hundred twenty-one for additional ideas.

(For Example, for your *verse*, you might want to use a plain tonic chord and go to a suspended chord (C to Csus4) and in your *chorus*, you might want to use 7th chords or a descending bass/left hand line (C, G/B, Am, G F, C/E, Dm, G7, C, etc.)

EXERCISE #3:

Create a song by choosing a standard blues progression or the I, vi, IV, V, I progression.

See if you can create differences between the sections of your songs.

CADENCES

A cadence, in a musical phrase, tells the listener whether or not the song is going to either continue or come to an end. We can compare this to writing (or speaking!) and the use of punctuation. Some sentences might use a comma, as a way of creating a pause. Other sentences might use a period to create the end of the phrase. A pause is not as strong as a period.

This concept is true in music too in that there are "strong" and "weak" cadences depending on the chords we choose to use. Some chords tell our ear to keep listening and some chords tell us that we've reached the end of that musical phrase. Some chords tell us that we've reached the end of the song.

Here is a list of cadences that you can put to good use in your songs:

1. Full Cadence: this is a strong cadence. It ends and resolves to the tonic. (In the key of C, we would resolve to C.) We can think of this as the end of the sentence. (I)

2. Half Cadence: finishes away from the tonic (as on the V chord, which in the key of C would be G). With V, we have gone away from the tonic. It's a pause; we can think of it like a comma in our phrase, instead of the conclusion of the sentence. (V)

3. Deceptive Cadence: does not resolve on the tonic. It can feel "unexpected" (fresh!) and is much less resolved than the full cadence. A deceptive cadence is when the V chord resolves to a chord other than the tonic (I). For example, we might go to the vi (C to Am, in the key of C.) This is a typical deceptive cadence. Or, we might also go to VI (C to A major). This is a surprise ending to our sentence. (vi or VI)

4. Plagal Cadence: we go from IV to I, instead of from V to I (F to C in the key of C major, instead of G to C). This is sometimes called the "amen" cadence. (See if you can hear the "amen" of a choir when you play this cadence!) (IV – I)

- ♪ Cadences are a great way to link contrasting sections together.
- ♪ Cadences can be used in the verse to lead us easily into the next section.
- ♪ Cadences can be repeated with the words of the title over them in the chorus.

What is a substitution chord?

It is a chord that shares a common tone with your original chord.

A chord can be "substituted" for another chord when it contains at least one note (called a common tone) that is shared with the original chord.

If you want to find some different chords than the ones you're using, this is a great way to come up with new and interesting chords for your progressions.

What common tones are shared between the F major chord and the A minor chord?

SUBSTITUTIONS

On the next page, you will find examples of some major and minor triad chords for substitutions. The chords can be found by looking for common tones.

(Note: We probably wouldn't use a substitution chord for I right off the bat in a song; otherwise, our ears wouldn't know where they were and where they had started from. This is just a basic chart to get the juices flowing for creativity.)

These are chords that you can use in the key of C and with the following chord progression:

I – IV – V – I (C – F – G – C)

Substitutions

More Basic Major/Minor Triad Chords for use
in Substitutions -- Using Common Tones

Let's use this progression: I - IV - V - I (or for example, in the key of C: C - F - G - C)

1. C chord and Substitution Possibilities

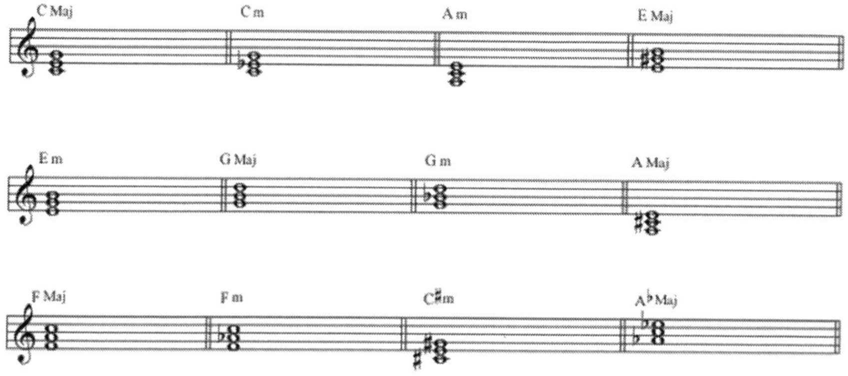

2. F chord and Substitution Possibilities

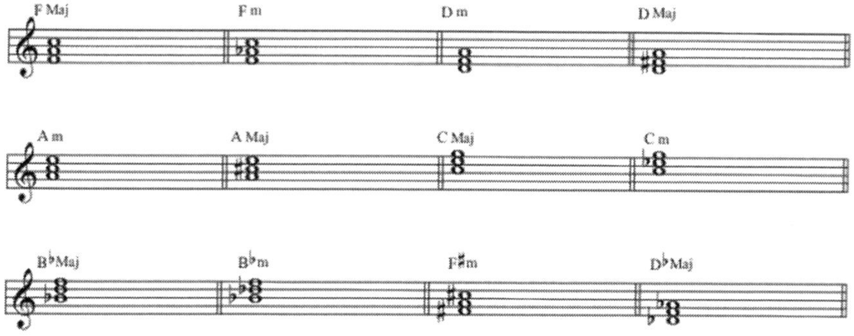

3. G chord and Substitution Possibilities

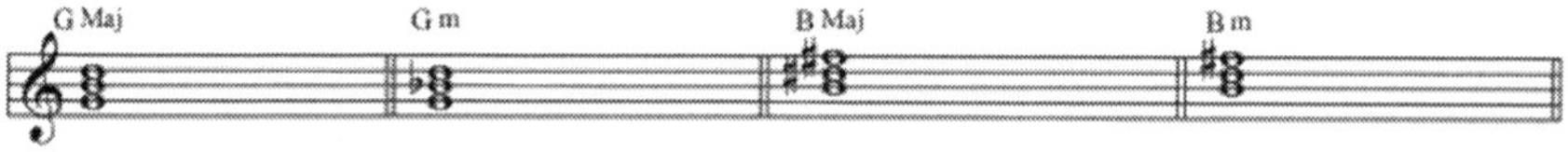

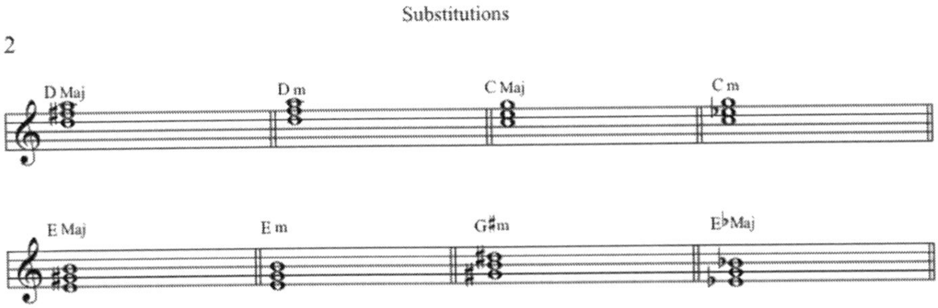

We can also play around with "surprise" chords that are not contained within the scale.

These are some chords that you might like to try using in a particular major key to see what you can come up with:

1. The Major II (in the key of C, this would be D Maj, instead of Dm)

2. The Major III (in the key of C, this would be E Maj, instead of Em)

3. The minor iv (using an Fm chord in the key of C)

4. The Major VI (in the key of C, this would be A Maj, instead of Am)

5. The ♭VI (using an A♭ chord in the key of C)

6. ♭VII (using a B♭ Maj chord in the key of C)

...and for minor keys, you might like to explore some of these chord ideas:

1. II (in the key of Am, this would be B Maj)
2. ♭II (in the key of Am, this would be B♭ Maj)
3. ii (in the key of Am, this would be Bm)
4. IV (in the key of Am, this would be D Maj)
5. I (in the key of Am, this would be A Maj)

We can hear a lot of elaborate, extended chords and more complicated progressions in older standard popular songs, as well as jazz and rhythm and blues tunes, etc.

There is a ton of great information out there on jazz harmony and theory. Jazz teachers and classes are also available and can get you started in a much better and more detailed way than I can cover here in this book on songwriting. I love to appreciate and listen to jazz music. However, I am not a jazz player by *any* stretch of the imagination—so for me, that world is a bird of another feather and a completely different breed of cat! ☺ Definitely on my bucket-list for study though, I have to say.

We can also add 7th notes to our basic three-note triad to create major 7th chords, minor 7th chords, and dominant 7th chords. We can add the 6th (of the scale) to the chord for extra color. We can use suspensions (when one or more notes are temporarily held before resolving to a chord tone) as well.

Use your ear, mess around, make your own choices, and decide what you like!

More Ways to Add to, or to Change Chords

1. Use the V7 (dominant 7th) chord in your progressions to add color or a "bluesy" quality

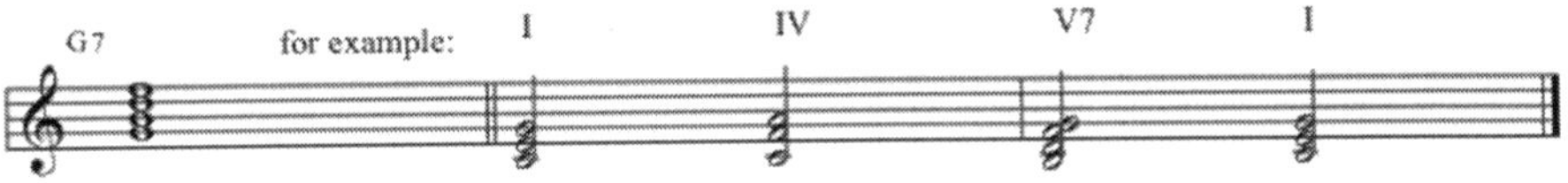

2. Common ways we can add to or change chords:

EXERCISE: Switch back & forth between 2 variations of a chord to create 4 bars of a groove. For example:

Try different chords and different "inversions" (take a look at inversions in the next example). Inversions are numbered in the order their bass tones would appear in a closed root position chord (from bottom to top).

Experiment; do some more noodling and see what happens. Determine what sounds good to your ear.

Fun Experiments With Chords

1. Play around with different inversions of your chord progressions and see what inversions move the most easily as you progress to the next chord in your song. Just see what you like!

root position | 1st inversion | 2nd inversion

2. Try lowering the 3rd of your Major Chord by 1/2 step (to create a minor chord.)

3. Explore some suspensions.

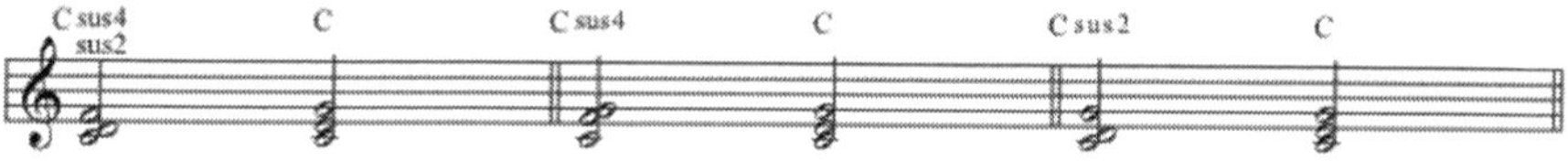

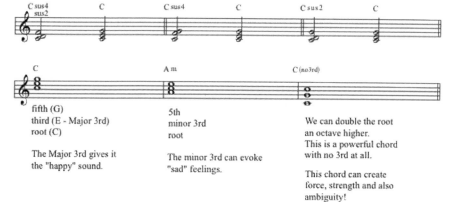

fifth (G)
third (E - Major 3rd)
root (C)

The Major 3rd gives it the "happy" sound.

5th
minor 3rd
root

The minor 3rd can evoke "sad" feelings.

We can double the root an octave higher.
This is a powerful chord with no 3rd at all.

This chord can create force, strength and also ambiguity!

EXERCISE:

Make up 3 different chord progressions using these 3 different kinds of chords:
1. inversions
2. major/minor chords
3. suspensions

See what kinds of emotions they suggest. Discover what kinds of song lyrics they inspire you to think about.

EXERCISE:

Take a basic progression:

1. For example: I – IV – V – I (In the key of C: C – F – G – C)
2. Or maybe: I – vi – ii – V – I (In the key of C: C – Am – Dm – G – C)
3. Experiment with substitution chords for your progression. Try and find lots of different choices.
4. See if any of those progressions with your substitution chords could be something you would like to work with in a song.

EXERCISE:

Listen to a bunch of songs on the radio or iTunes. See if you can listen for:

1. Mostly triads
2. 7th chords
3. More extended, involved chords

CREATING SIMPLE 8 BAR CHORD PROGRESSIONS

For a simple 8 bar chord progression, we can create a triad on the 1st note of a C scale (C), then on the 4th note of the scale (F), and then, back to the

1st note (C), up to the 5th note (G), and back to the 1st note (C), to the 4th note (F) to the 5th note (G), and back to the 1st note again (C).

Creating Simple 8 Bar Chord Progressions

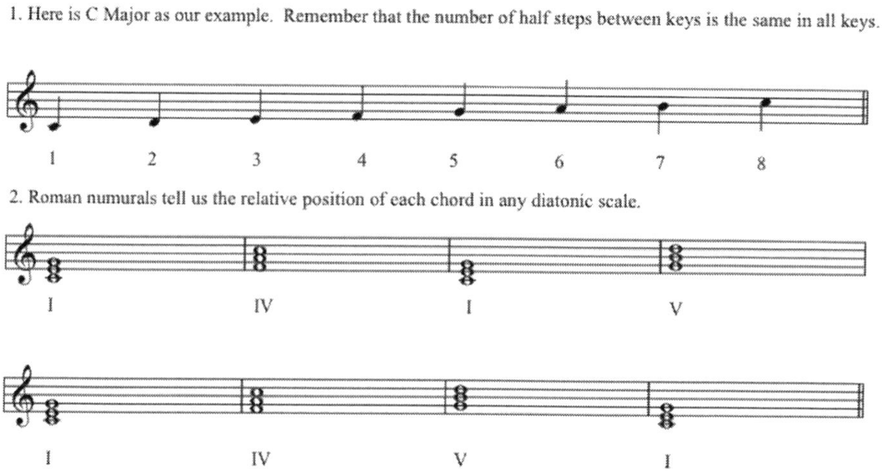
1. Here is C Major as our example. Remember that the number of half steps between keys is the same in all keys.
1 2 3 4 5 6 7 8
2. Roman numurals tell us the relative position of each chord in any diatonic scale.
I IV I V
I IV V I

1. Take a look at C major in the example. Remember that the number of half steps between notes is the same in all keys.

2. Roman numerals tell us the relative position of each chord in any diatonic scale.

EXERCISE:

Transpose this chord progression:

I – IV – I – V – I – IV – V – I
(C – F – C – G – C – F – G – C) into these keys:
D, A, and E♭.

(You can take a look at all of these scales/modes in all twelve keys at the end of the chapter!)

REVIEW

Each major diatonic scale has a relative minor scale that shares the same key signature. We find the starting note of the relative minor scale by counting down three half steps. (For example, the relative minor of C major is A minor.)

Check out some of the scales and modes again and see if you can take advantage of all these different scales and keys to create various moods and emotions in your songs. Keep in mind too, that you can use very simple triads to create amazing songs.

EXERCISE:

1. Experiment with scales and chord progressions!
2. See if any scales seem brighter, more dramatic, warmer, more neutral, soft, or forceful to you.
3. See if they start to suggest any creative ideas for you.

SUMMARY on enriching chords with color and spice:

Without going heavily into jazz chords, here are some simple approaches for modifying or supplementing chords in popular songs:

1. Major chords—add 2, add 6, or a Major 7th. We can also change a note by forming a sus2 or sus4 (no 3rd).
2. Minor chords—add 2, add 6, or a minor 7th. We can also change a note by creating a minor sus4 (no 3rd).
3. We can make a dominant 7th chord or a dominant 7 sus4 (V7 sus4) (no 3rd).
4. Open 5ths (chords with no 3rd, just root and 5th)—we can also supplement a sus2 with the open 5ths.

SUMMARY: "Reminder List" of some scales and modes to take a look at for creativity:

1. Major scale
2. Natural minor
3. Melodic minor
4. Harmonic minor
5. Dorian
6. Phrygian
7. Lydian
8. Mixolydian
9. Aeolian
10. Ionian (Major scale...so: #1!)

Here are the scales/modes as listed in the previous summary (including a couple of blues scales as well) in all twelve keys:

Major, Minor Scales, Modes & Blues

(In these cases, we'll be looking at C as our starting point)

The Major Scale - (so, C major): **

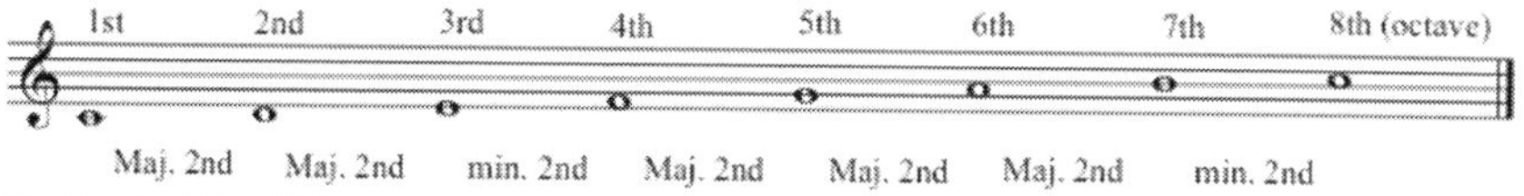

The Relative Natural Minor

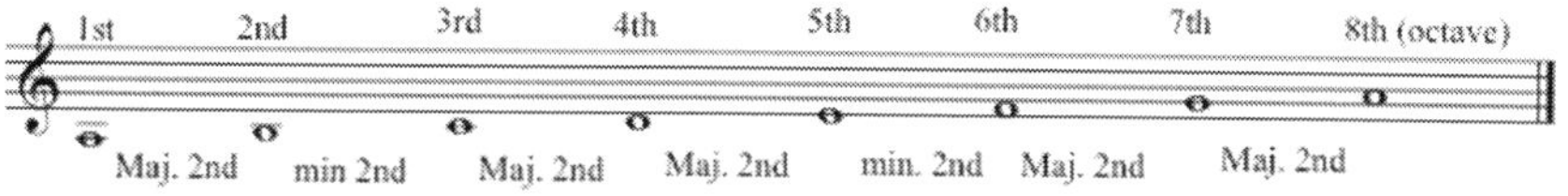

The melodic minor - has maj. 6th and maj. 7th (leading note) going up; a min. 7th and min. 6th going down)

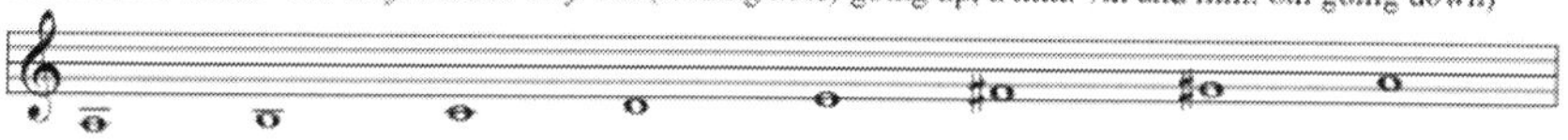

The harmonic minor - has min. 6th and the leading note (maj. 7th) going both up and down.

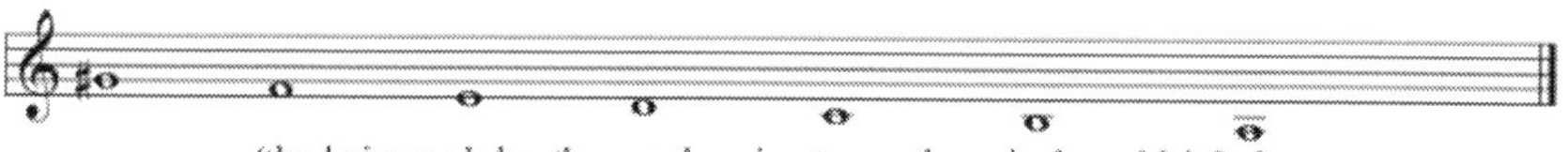

Dorian mode

(the dorian mode has the same key signature as the major key a Maj. 2nd below the starting note of the dorian scale. For example C dorian shares the same key signature as Bb Maj. (two flats - Bb, Eb)

** you can count the intervals in all of these scales in the same way that I have illustrated in the first two scales.

Scales, Modes, Blues

2

Mixolydian Mode (the Mixolydian mode has the same key signature as the major key a Perfect 4th up the starting note of the Mixolydian scale.

Phrygian (the Phrygian mode has the same key signature as the major key a Maj. 3rd down from the starting note of the Phrygian scale.

Lydian (the Lydian mode has the same key signature as the major key a Perfect 5th up from the starting note of the Lydian scale.

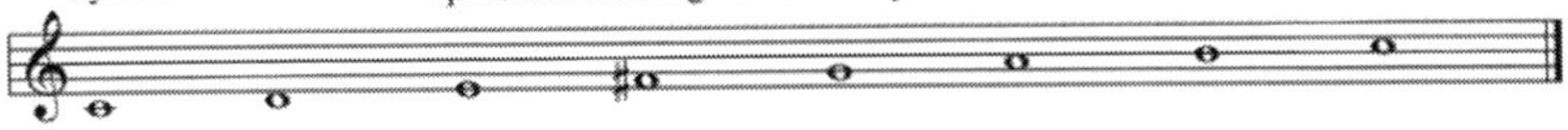

Aeolian (aka: a natural minor scale; same key signature as the key 3 half steps above, in this case, Eb Maj.)

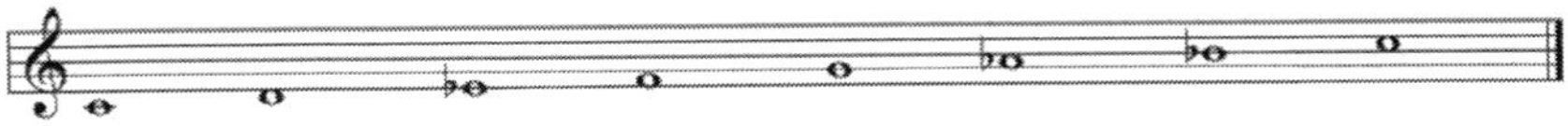

Ionian (aka: Major scale)

Blues (C min. blues)

Blues ("ragtime"/major)

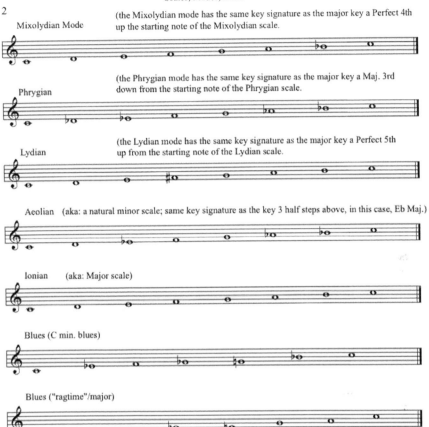

Major, Minor Scales, Modes & Blues

(In these cases, we'll be looking at Db (or C#) as our starting point)

The Major Scale - (so, Db major): **

Maj. 2nd Maj. 2nd min. 2nd Maj. 2nd Maj. 2nd Maj. 2nd min. 2nd

The Relative Natural Minor

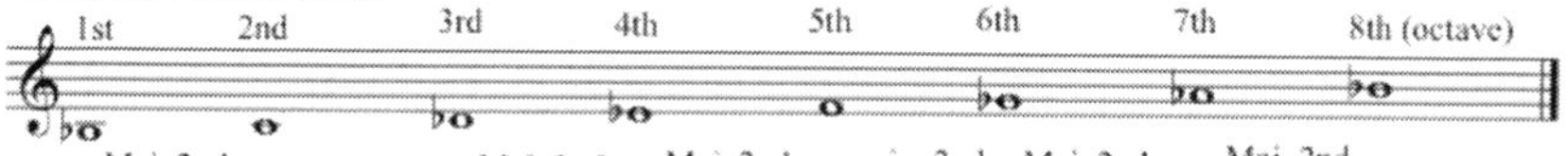

Maj. 2nd min 2nd Maj. 2nd Maj. 2nd min. 2nd Maj. 2nd Maj. 2nd

The melodic minor - has maj. 6th and maj. 7th (leading note) going up; a min. 7th and min. 6th going down)

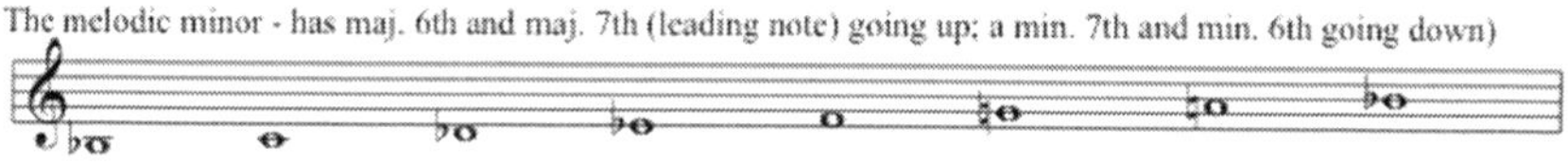

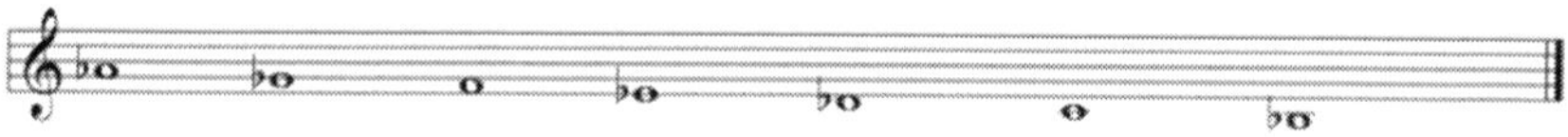

The harmonic minor - has min. 6th and the leading note (maj. 7th) going both up and down.

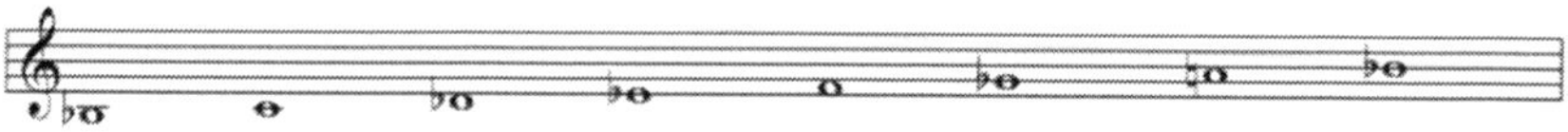

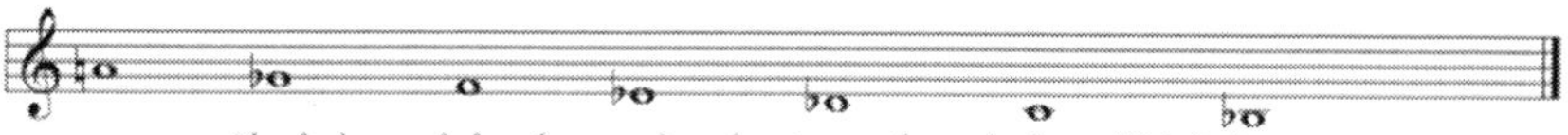

Dorian mode (the dorian mode has the same key signature as the major key a Maj. 2nd below the starting note of the dorian scale. For example Db dorian shares the same key signature as B Maj. - 5#'s (therefore, enharmonically, we will start on C#, etc.)

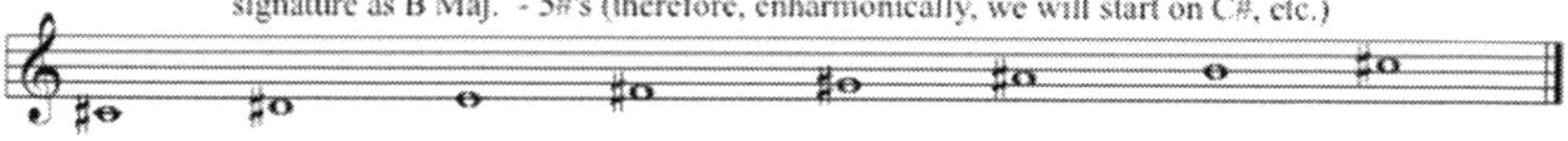

** you can count the intervals in all of these scales in the same way that I have illustrated in the first two scales.

Scales, Modes, Blues

2

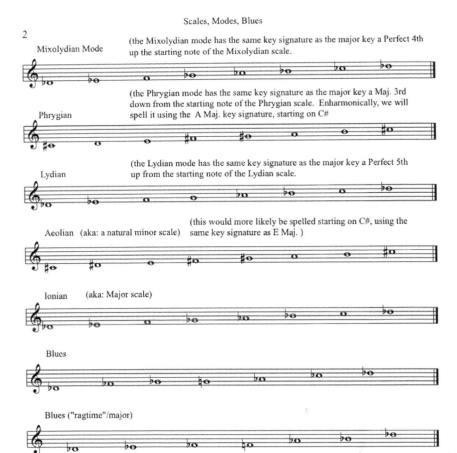

Mixolydian Mode

(the Mixolydian mode has the same key signature as the major key a Perfect 4th up the starting note of the Mixolydian scale.

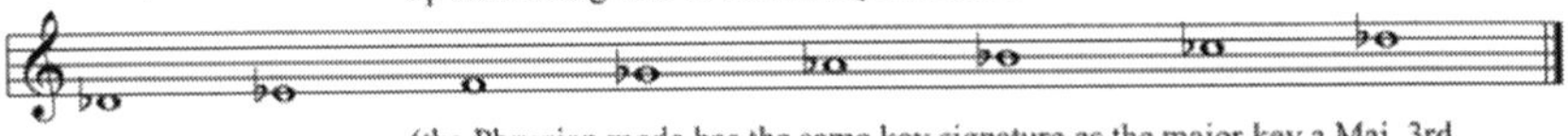

Phrygian

(the Phrygian mode has the same key signature as the major key a Maj. 3rd down from the starting note of the Phrygian scale. Enharmonically, we will spell it using the A Maj. key signature, starting on C#

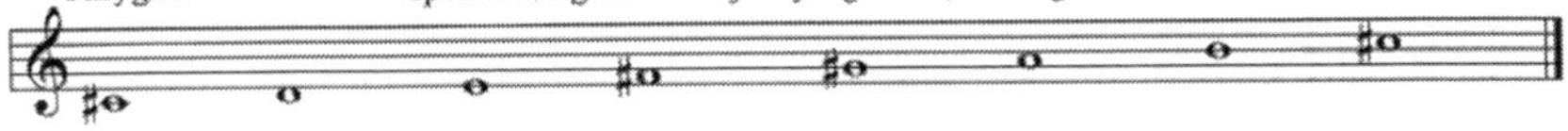

Lydian

(the Lydian mode has the same key signature as the major key a Perfect 5th up from the starting note of the Lydian scale.

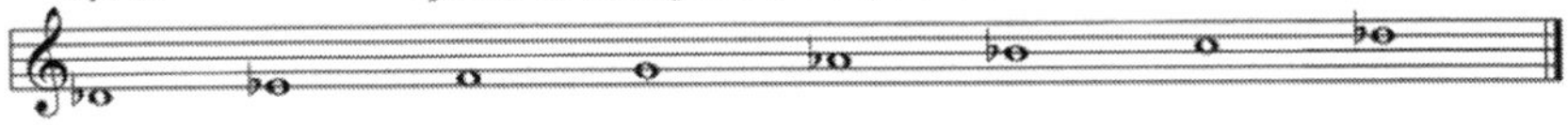

Aeolian (aka: a natural minor scale)

(this would more likely be spelled starting on C#, using the same key signature as E Maj.)

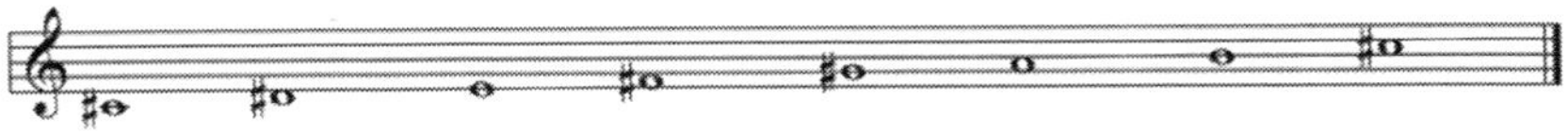

Ionian (aka: Major scale)

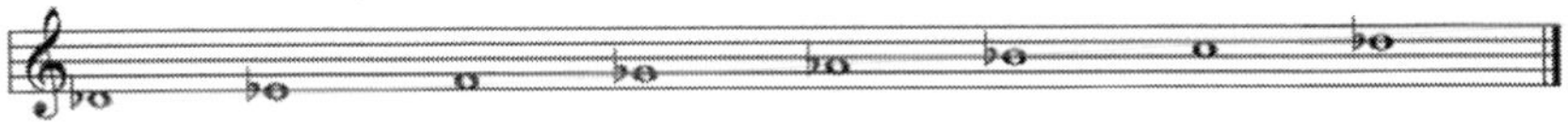

Blues

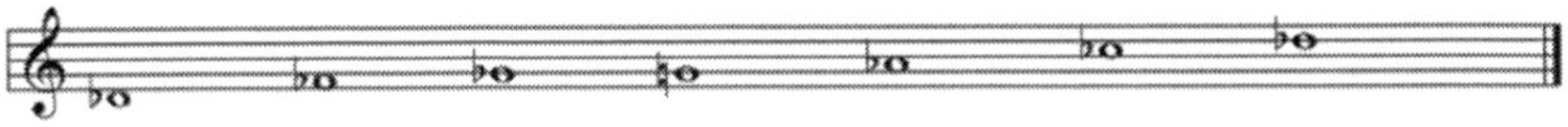

Blues ("ragtime"/major)

Major, Minor Scales, Modes & Blues

(In these cases, we'll be looking at D as our starting point)

The Major Scale - (so, D major): **

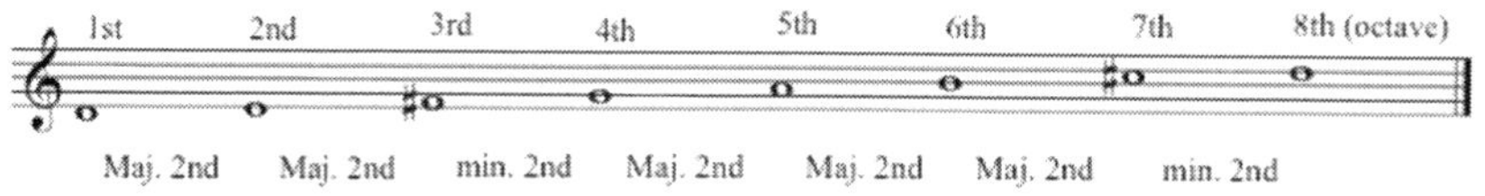

The Relative Natural Minor

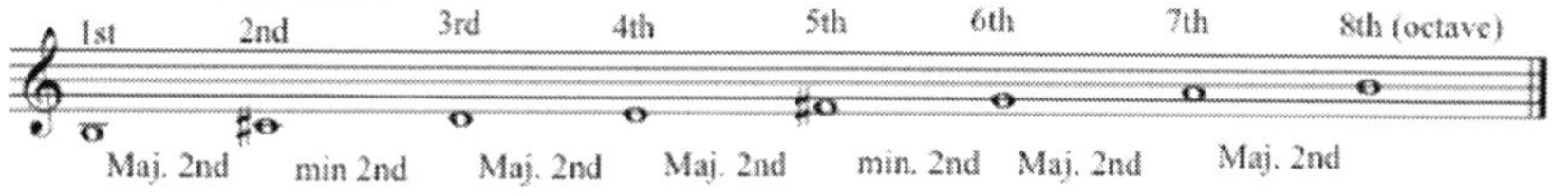

The melodic minor - has maj. 6th and maj. 7th (leading note) going up; a min. 7th and min. 6th going down)

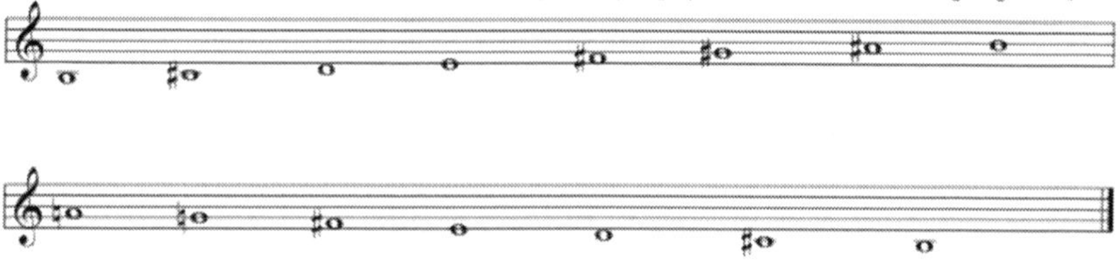

The harmonic minor - has min. 6th and the leading note (maj. 7th) going both up and down.

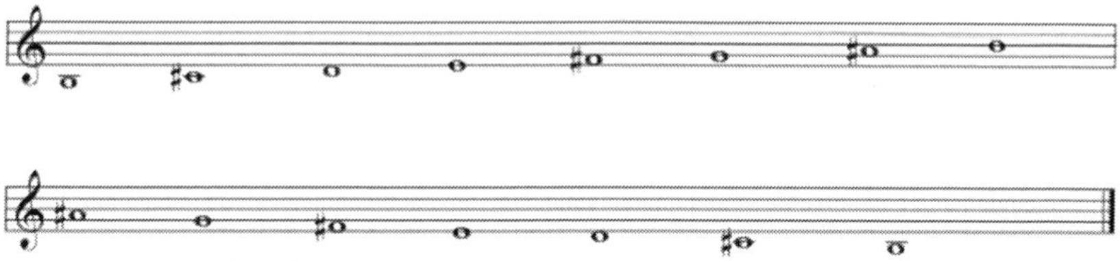

Dorian mode (the dorian mode has the same key signature as the major key a Maj. 2nd below the starting note of the dorian scale. For example D dorian shares the same key signature as C Maj.)

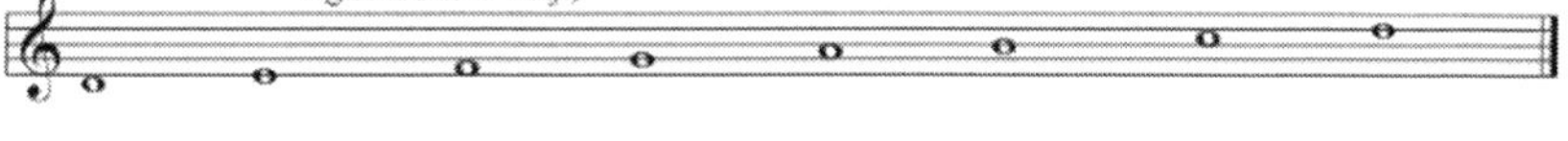

** you can count the intervals in all of these scales in the same way that I have illustrated in the first two scales.

Scales, Modes, Blues

2

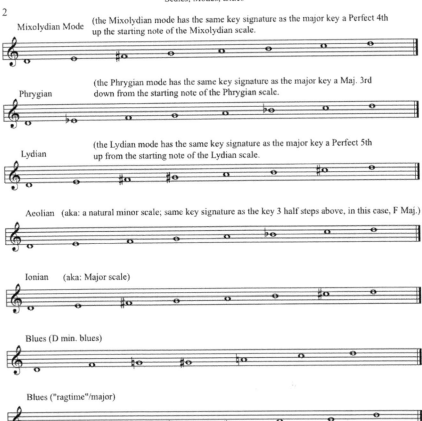

Mixolydian Mode (the Mixolydian mode has the same key signature as the major key a Perfect 4th up the starting note of the Mixolydian scale.

Phrygian (the Phrygian mode has the same key signature as the major key a Maj. 3rd down from the starting note of the Phrygian scale.

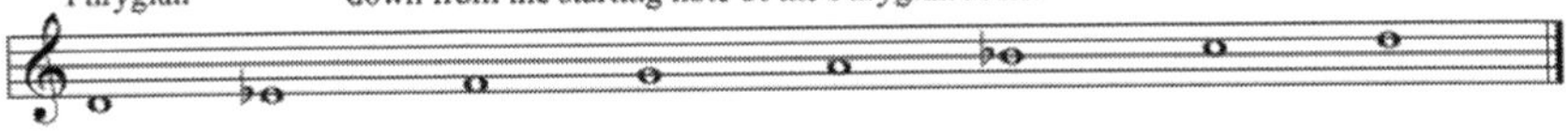

Lydian (the Lydian mode has the same key signature as the major key a Perfect 5th up from the starting note of the Lydian scale.

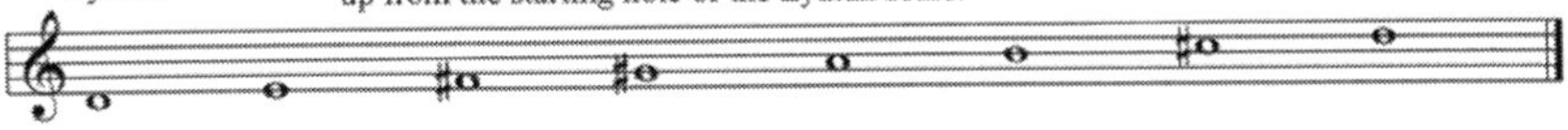

Aeolian (aka: a natural minor scale; same key signature as the key 3 half steps above, in this case, F Maj.)

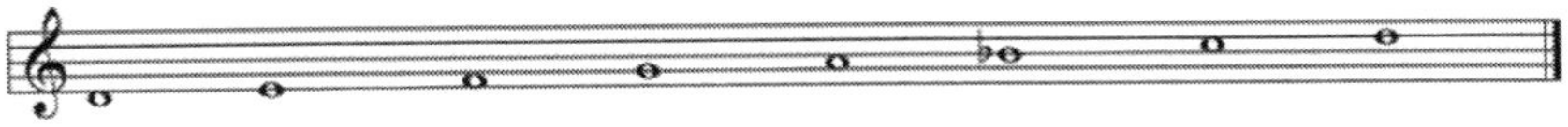

Ionian (aka: Major scale)

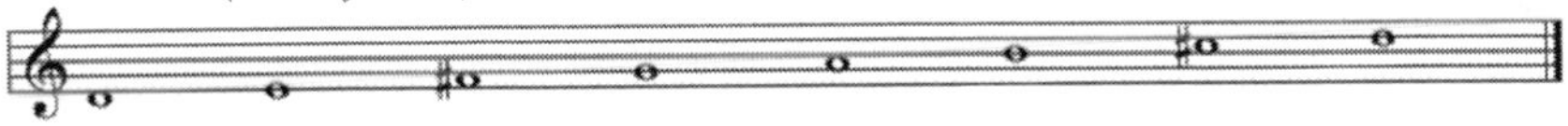

Blues (D min. blues)

Blues ("ragtime"/major)

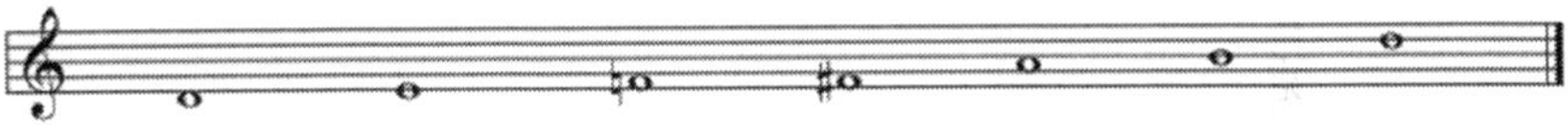

Major, Minor Scales, Modes & Blues

(In these cases, we'll be looking at Eb as our starting point)

The Major Scale - (so, Eb major):**

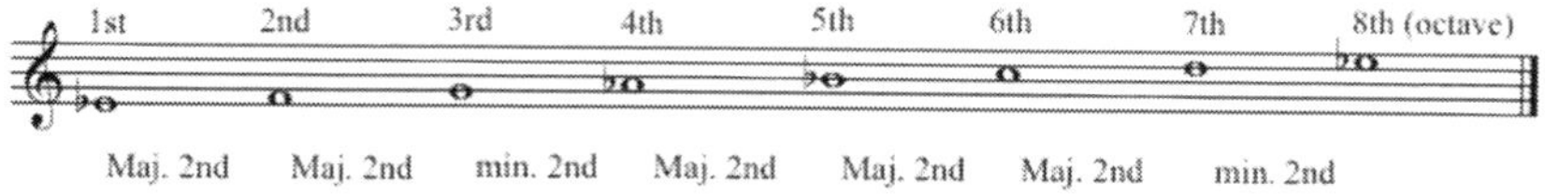

The Relative Natural Minor

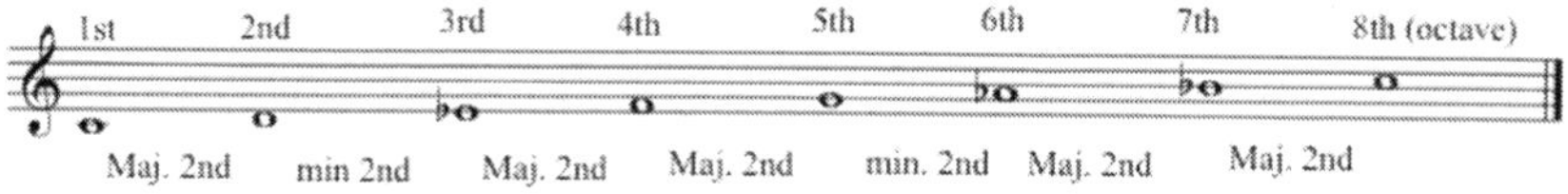

The melodic minor - has maj. 6th and maj. 7th (leading note) going up; a min. 7th and min. 6th going down)

The harmonic minor - has min. 6th and the leading note (maj. 7th) going both up and down.

Dorian mode (the dorian mode has the same key signature as the major key a Maj. 2nd below the starting note of the dorian scale. For example Eb dorian shares the same key signature as Db Maj.)

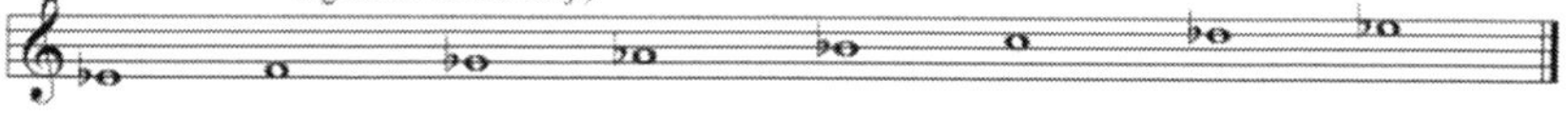

** you can count the intervals in all of these scales in the same way that I have illustrated in the first two scales.

Scales, Modes, Blues

2

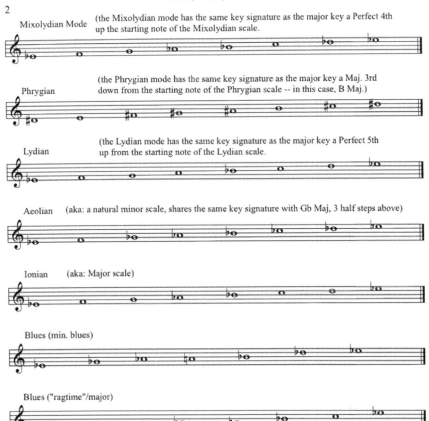

Mixolydian Mode (the Mixolydian mode has the same key signature as the major key a Perfect 4th up the starting note of the Mixolydian scale.

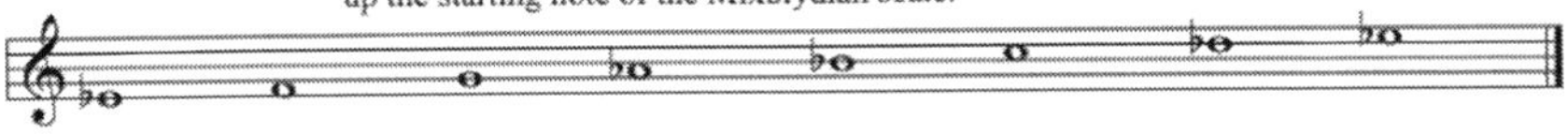

Phrygian (the Phrygian mode has the same key signature as the major key a Maj. 3rd down from the starting note of the Phrygian scale -- in this case, B Maj.)

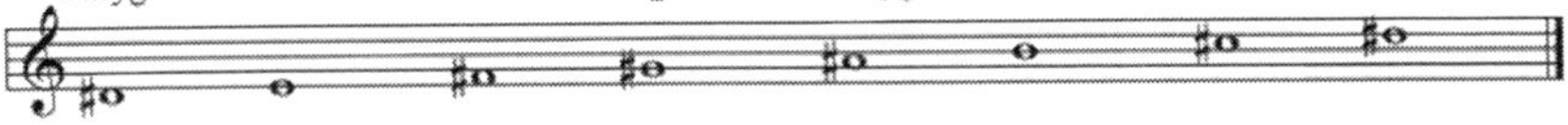

Lydian (the Lydian mode has the same key signature as the major key a Perfect 5th up from the starting note of the Lydian scale.

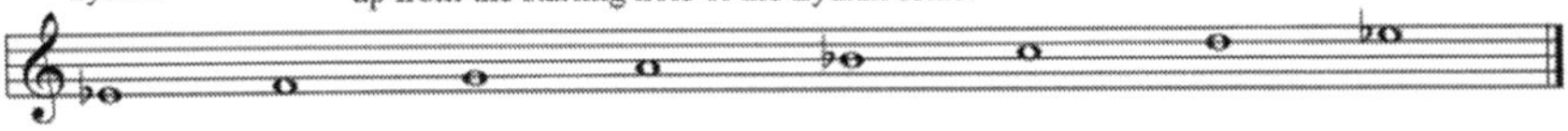

Aeolian (aka: a natural minor scale, shares the same key signature with Gb Maj, 3 half steps above)

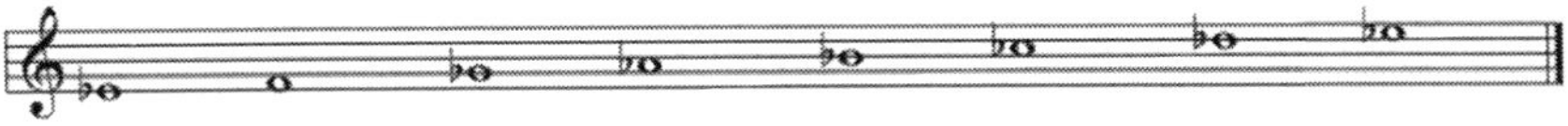

Ionian (aka: Major scale)

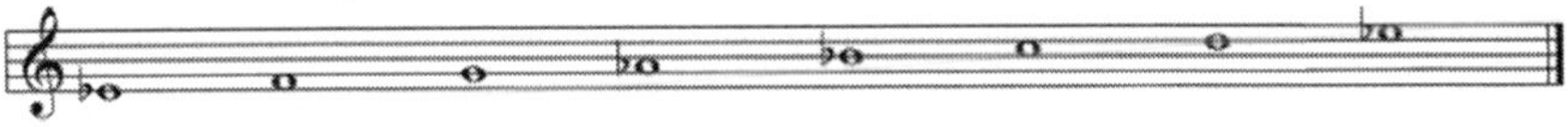

Blues (min. blues)

Blues ("ragtime"/major)

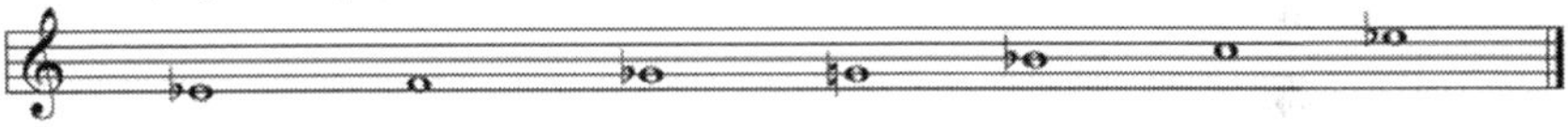

Major, Minor Scales, Modes & Blues

(In these cases, we'll be looking at E as our starting point)

The Major Scale - (so, E major): **

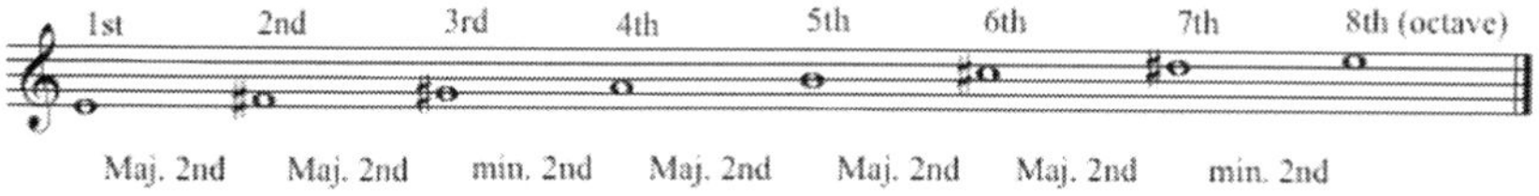

The Relative Natural Minor

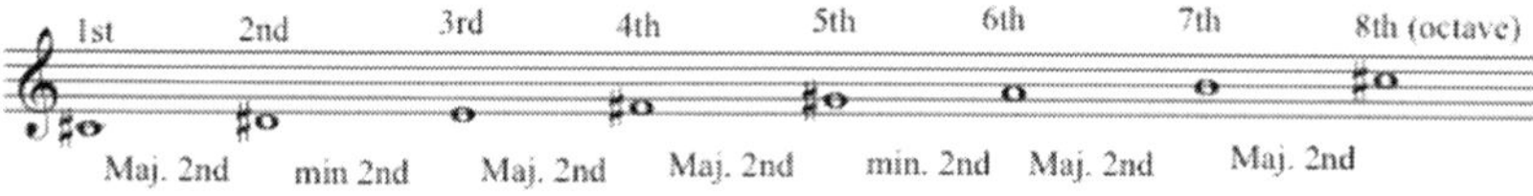

The melodic minor - has maj. 6th and maj. 7th (leading note) going up; a min. 7th and min. 6th going down)

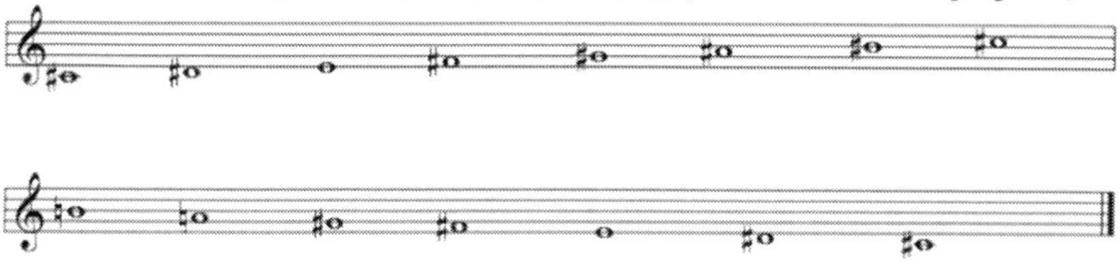

The harmonic minor - has min. 6th and the leading note (maj. 7th) going both up and down.

Dorian mode (the dorian mode has the same key signature as the major key a Maj. 2nd below the starting note of the dorian scale. For example E dorian shares the same key signature as D Maj.)

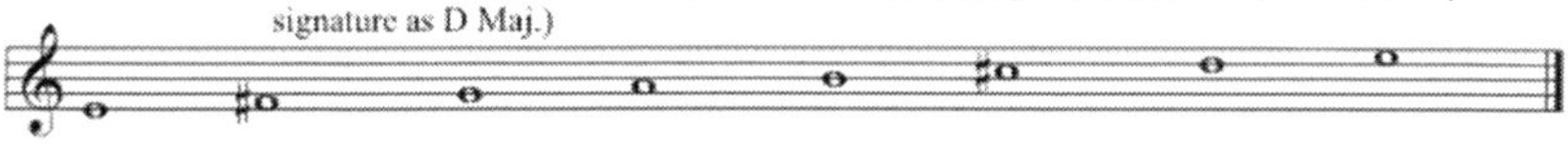

** you can count the intervals in all of these scales in the same way that I have illustrated in the first two scales.

Scales, Modes, Blues

2

Mixolydian Mode (the Mixolydian mode has the same key signature as the major key a Perfect 4th up the starting note of the Mixolydian scale.

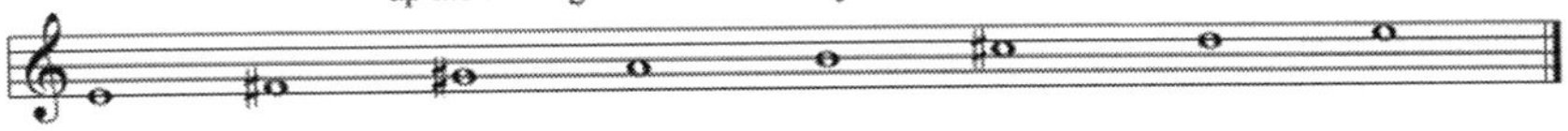

Phrygian (the Phrygian mode has the same key signature as the major key a Maj. 3rd down from the starting note of the Phrygian scale.

Lydian (the Lydian mode has the same key signature as the major key a Perfect 5th up from the starting note of the Lydian scale.

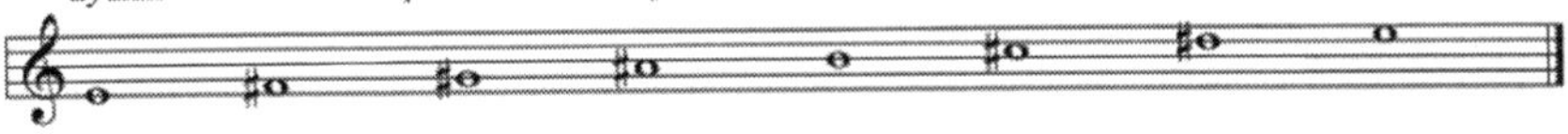

Aeolian (aka: a natural minor scale -- shares the same key signature as G Maj. -- 3 half steps up from E)

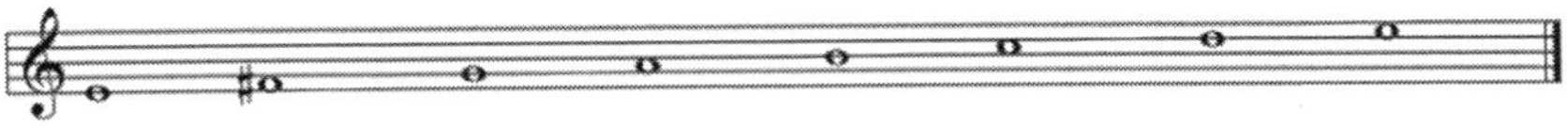

Ionian (aka: Major scale)

Blues (min. blues)

Blues ("ragtime"/major)

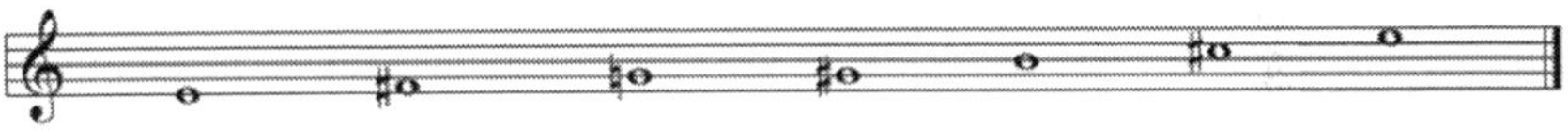

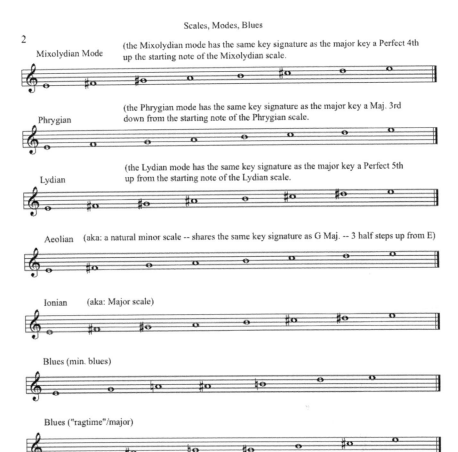

Major, Minor Scales, Modes & Blues

(In these cases, we'll be looking at F as our starting point)

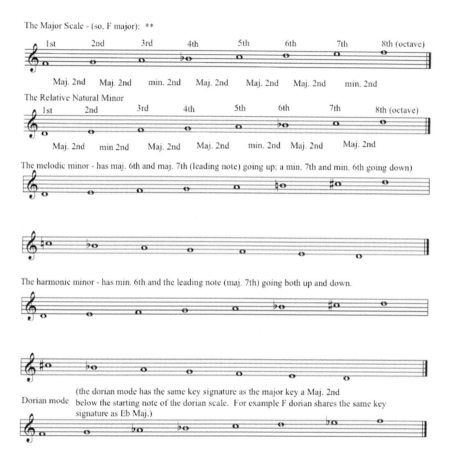

The Major Scale - (so, F major): **

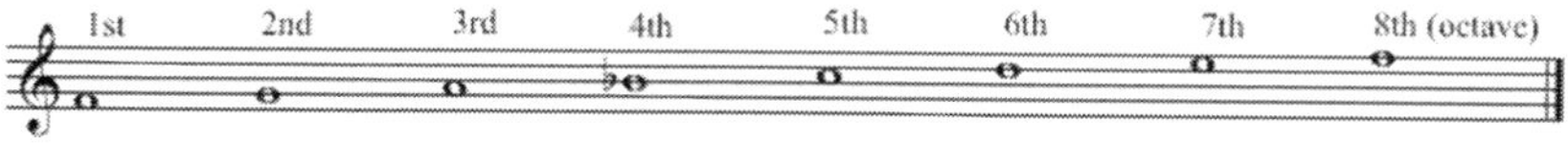

Maj. 2nd Maj. 2nd min. 2nd Maj. 2nd Maj. 2nd Maj. 2nd min. 2nd

The Relative Natural Minor

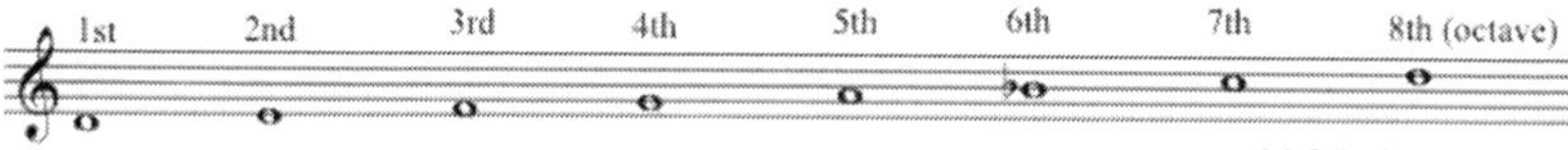

Maj. 2nd min 2nd Maj. 2nd Maj. 2nd min. 2nd Maj. 2nd Maj. 2nd

The melodic minor - has maj. 6th and maj. 7th (leading note) going up; a min. 7th and min. 6th going down)

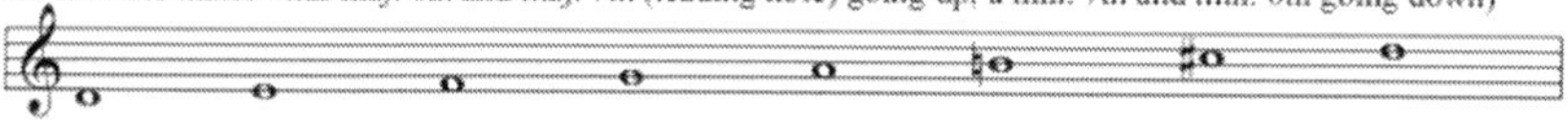

The harmonic minor - has min. 6th and the leading note (maj. 7th) going both up and down.

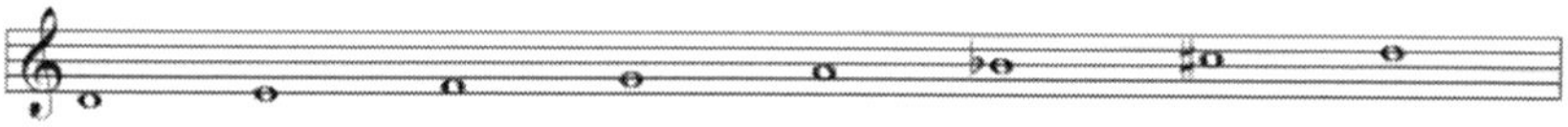

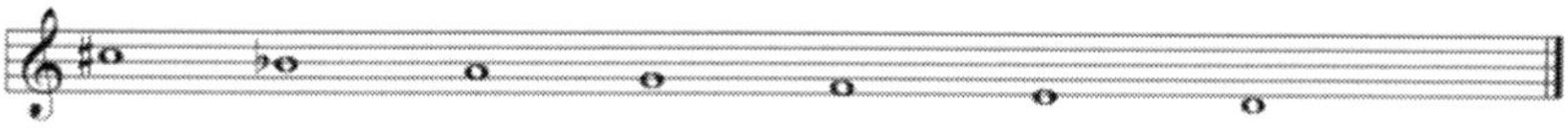

Dorian mode (the dorian mode has the same key signature as the major key a Maj. 2nd below the starting note of the dorian scale. For example F dorian shares the same key signature as Eb Maj.)

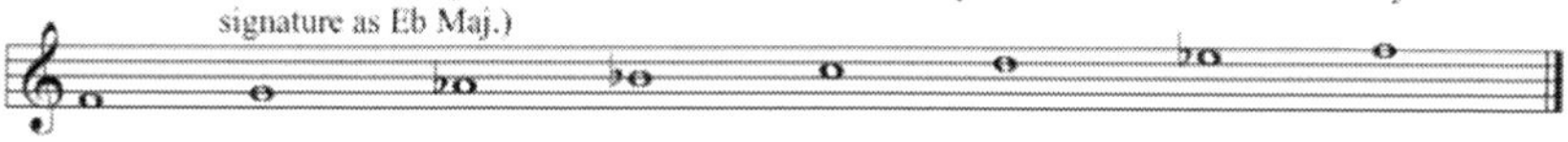

** you can count the intervals in all of these scales in the same way that I have illustrated in the first two scales.

Scales, Modes, Blues

2

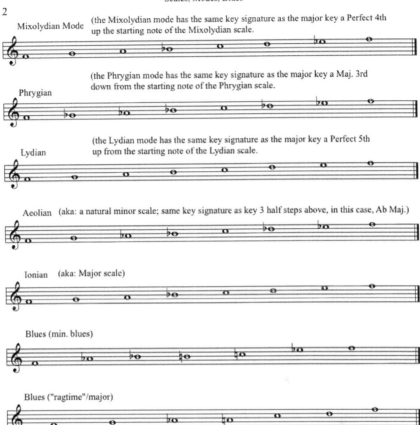

Mixolydian Mode (the Mixolydian mode has the same key signature as the major key a Perfect 4th up the starting note of the Mixolydian scale.

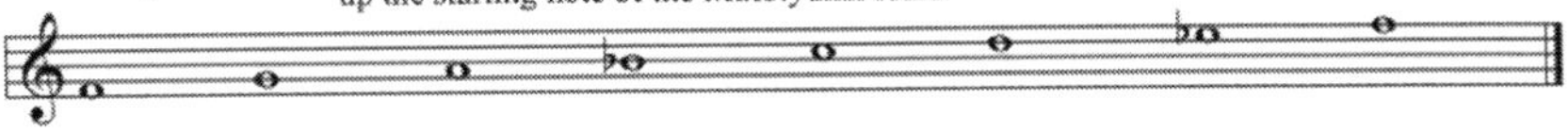

Phrygian (the Phrygian mode has the same key signature as the major key a Maj. 3rd down from the starting note of the Phrygian scale.

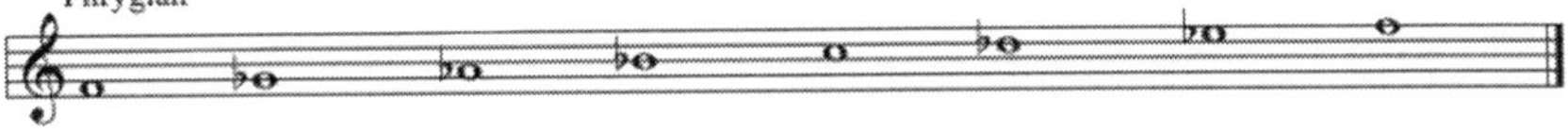

Lydian (the Lydian mode has the same key signature as the major key a Perfect 5th up from the starting note of the Lydian scale.

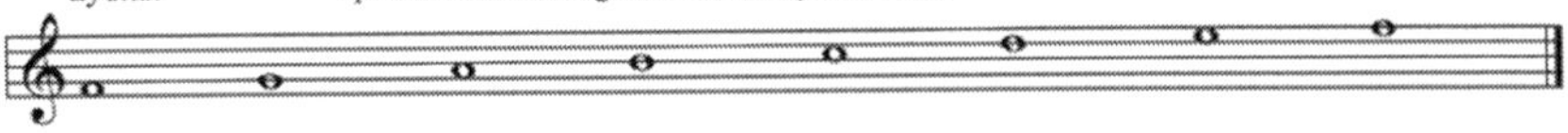

Aeolian (aka: a natural minor scale; same key signature as key 3 half steps above, in this case, Ab Maj.)

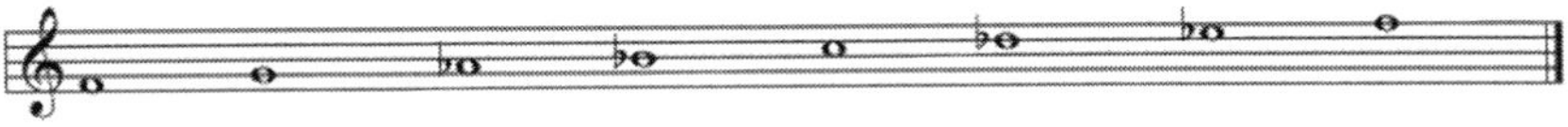

Ionian (aka: Major scale)

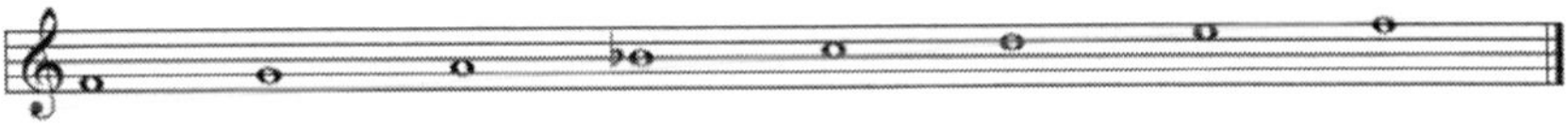

Blues (min. blues)

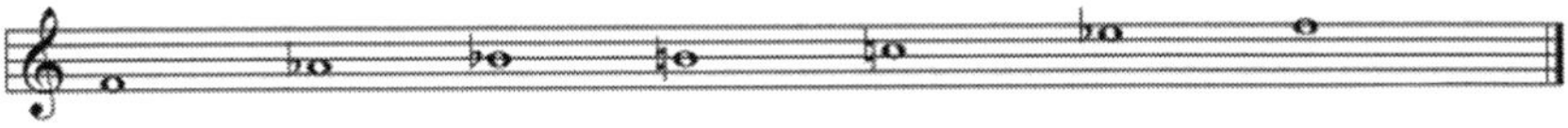

Blues ("ragtime"/major)

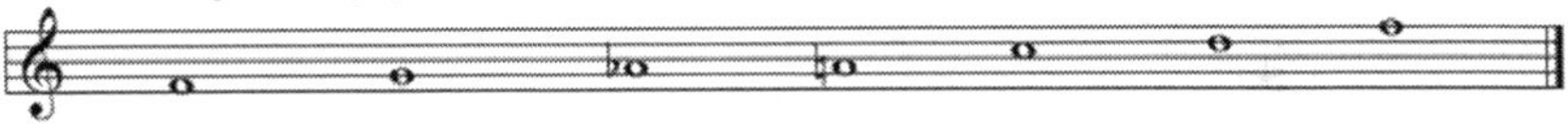

Major, Minor Scales, Modes & Blues

(In these cases, we'll be looking at Gb, or F# -- as our starting point)

The Major Scale - (so, Gb major):**

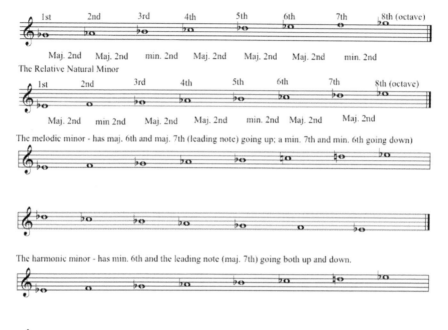

1st 2nd 3rd 4th 5th 6th 7th 8th (octave)

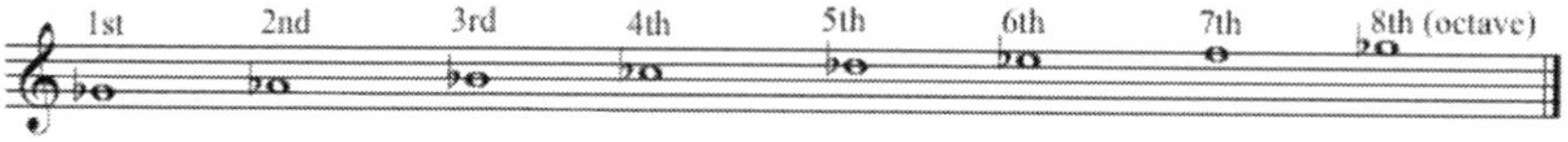

Maj. 2nd Maj. 2nd min. 2nd Maj. 2nd Maj. 2nd Maj. 2nd min. 2nd

The Relative Natural Minor

1st 2nd 3rd 4th 5th 6th 7th 8th (octave)

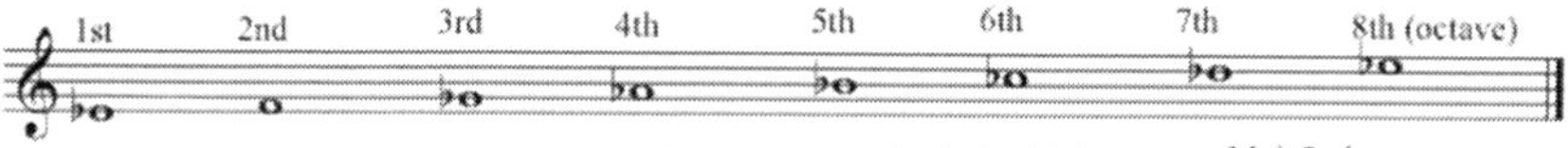

Maj. 2nd min 2nd Maj. 2nd Maj. 2nd min. 2nd Maj. 2nd Maj. 2nd

The melodic minor - has maj. 6th and maj. 7th (leading note) going up; a min. 7th and min. 6th going down)

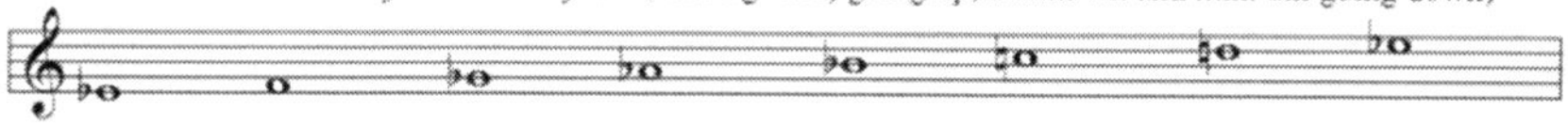

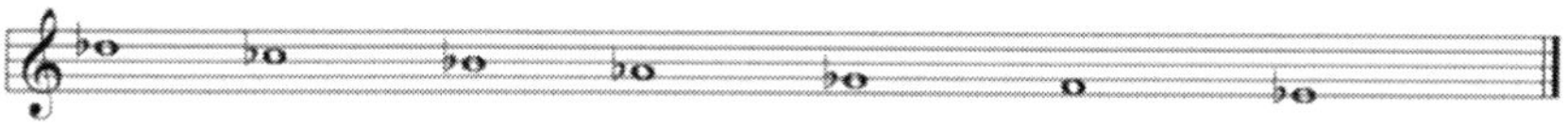

The harmonic minor - has min. 6th and the leading note (maj. 7th) going both up and down.

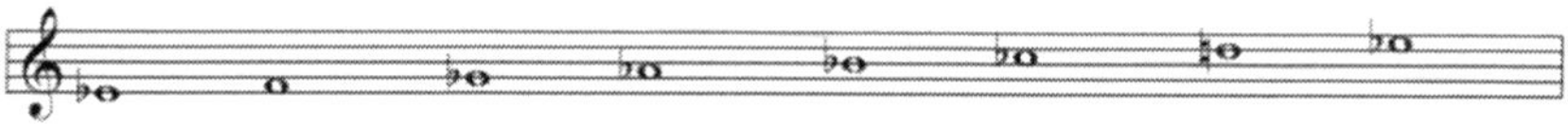

Dorian mode (the dorian mode has the same key signature as the major key a Maj. 2nd below the starting note of the dorian scale. For example F# dorian (enharmonic equivalent of Gb) shares the same key signature as E Maj.)

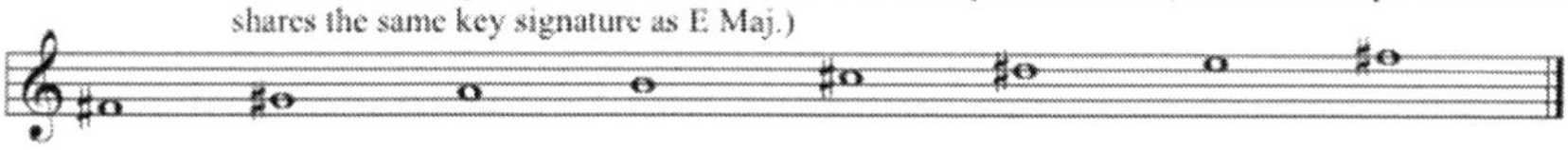

** you can count the intervals in all of these scales in the same way that I have illustrated in the first two scales.

Scales, Modes, Blues

2

Mixolydian Mode (the Mixolydian mode has the same key signature as the major key a Perfect 4th up the starting note of the Mixolydian scale.

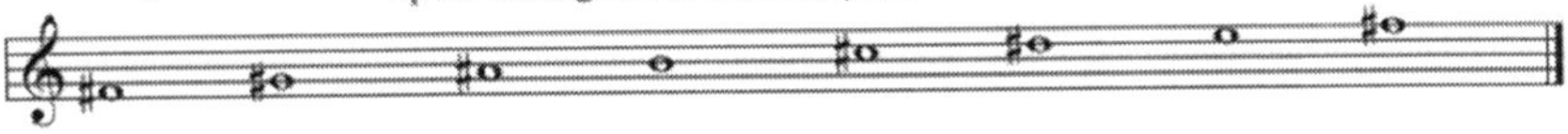

Phrygian (the Phrygian mode has the same key signature as the major key a Maj. 3rd down from the starting note of the Phrygian scale.

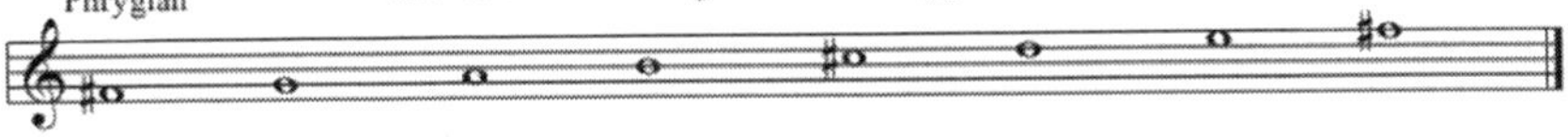

Lydian (the Lydian mode has the same key signature as the major key a Perfect 5th up from the starting note of the Lydian scale.

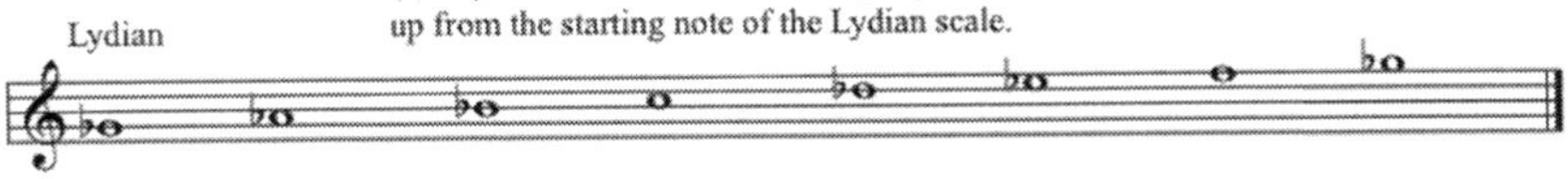

Aeolian (aka: a natural minor scale; same key signature as key 3 half steps above, in this case, A Maj.)

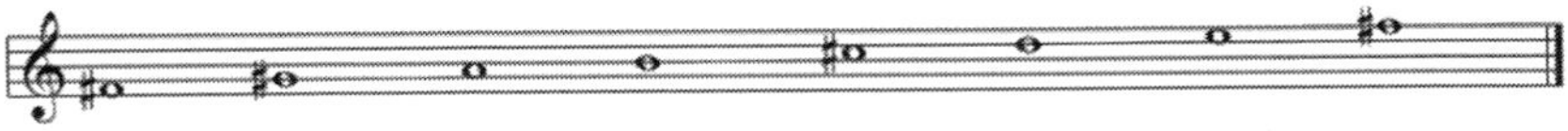

Ionian (aka: Major scale)

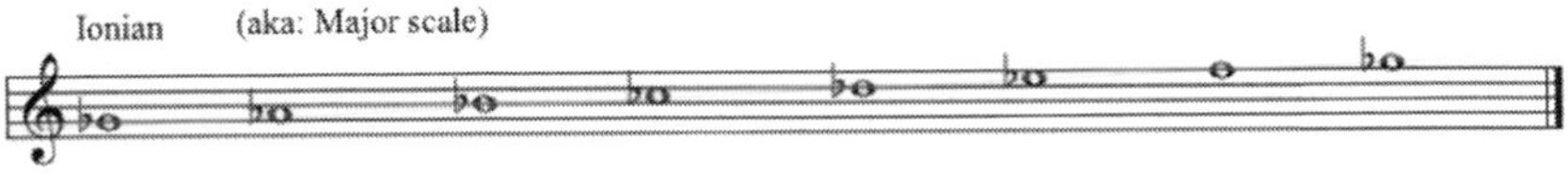

Blues (min. blues)

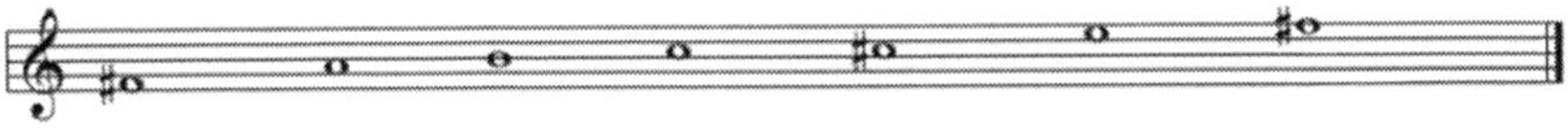

Blues ("ragtime"/major)

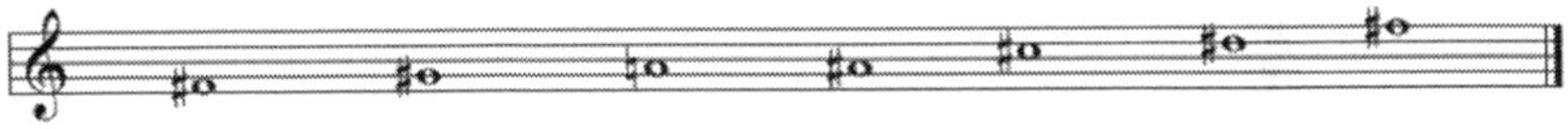

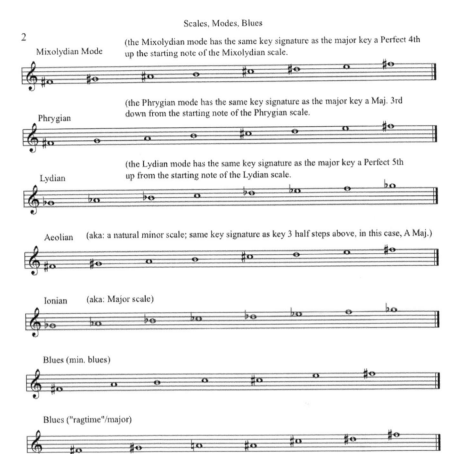

Major, Minor Scales, Modes & Blues

(In these cases, we'll be looking at G as our starting point)

The Major Scale - (so, G major): **

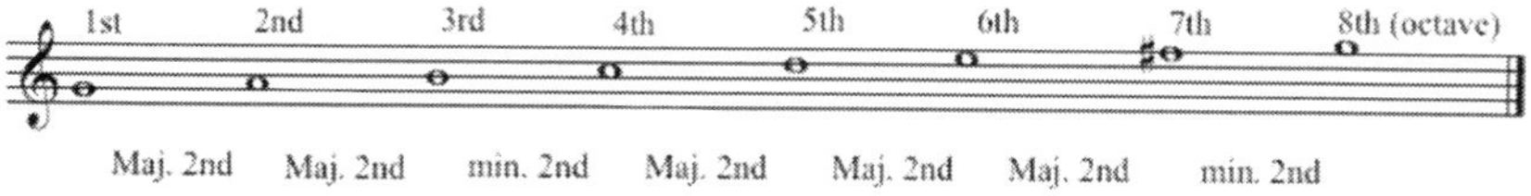

The Relative Natural Minor

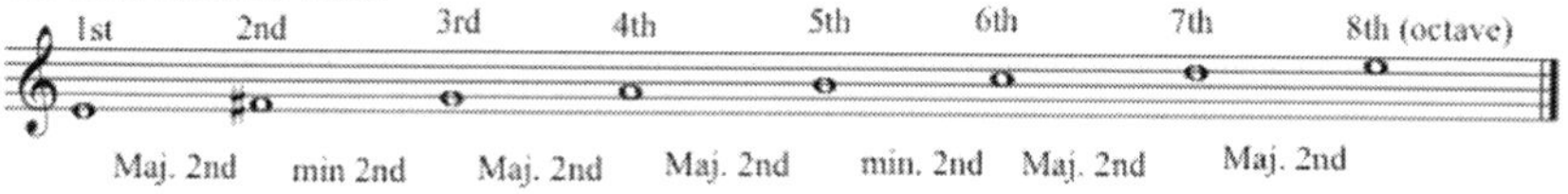

The melodic minor - has maj. 6th and maj. 7th (leading note) going up; a min. 7th and min. 6th going down)

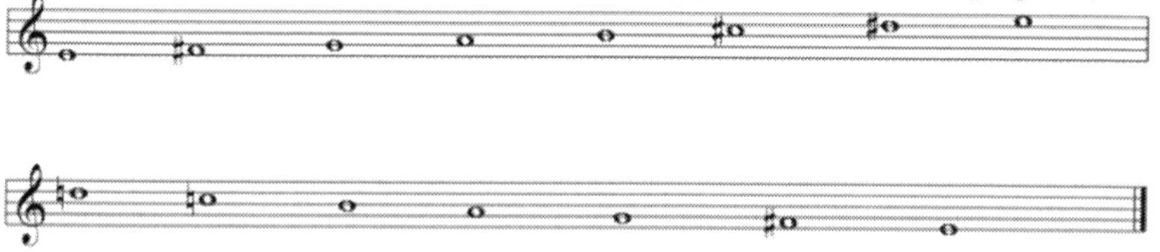

The harmonic minor - has min. 6th and the leading note (maj. 7th) going both up and down.

Dorian mode (the dorian mode has the same key signature as the major key a Maj. 2nd below the starting note of the dorian scale. For example G dorian shares the same key signature as F Maj.)

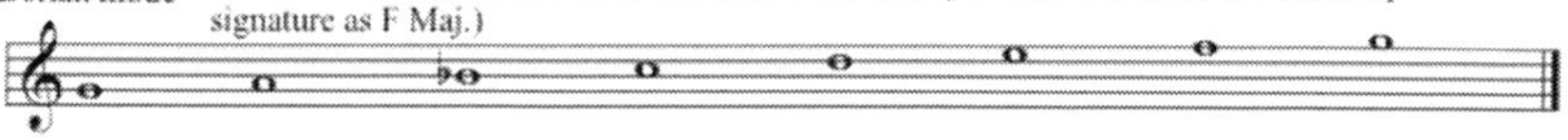

** you can count the intervals in all of these scales in the same way that I have illustrated in the first two scales.

Scales, Modes, Blues

2

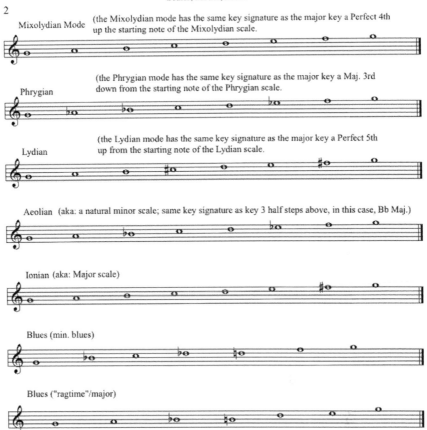

Mixolydian Mode (the Mixolydian mode has the same key signature as the major key a Perfect 4th up the starting note of the Mixolydian scale.

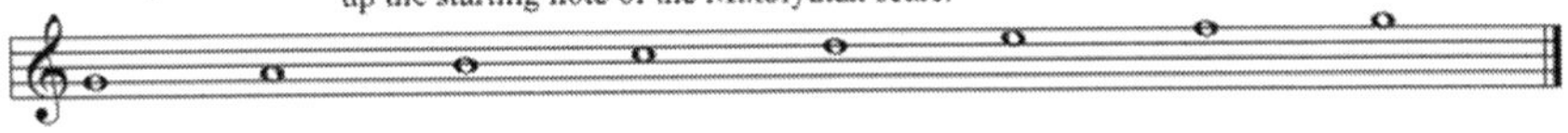

Phrygian (the Phrygian mode has the same key signature as the major key a Maj. 3rd down from the starting note of the Phrygian scale.

Lydian (the Lydian mode has the same key signature as the major key a Perfect 5th up from the starting note of the Lydian scale.

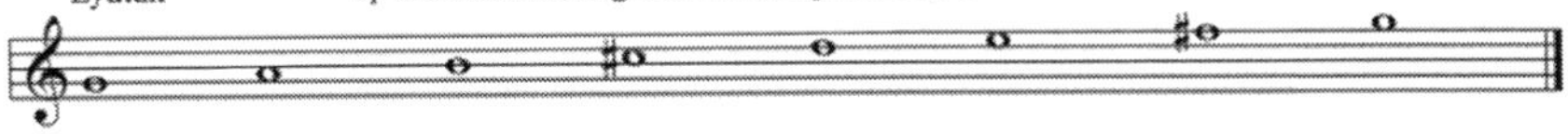

Aeolian (aka: a natural minor scale; same key signature as key 3 half steps above, in this case, Bb Maj.)

Ionian (aka: Major scale)

Blues (min. blues)

Blues ("ragtime"/major)

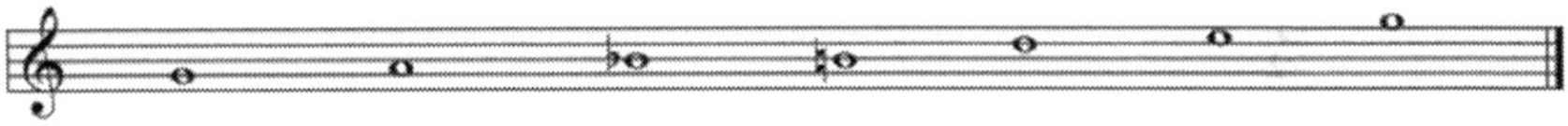

Major, Minor Scales, Modes & Blues

(In these cases, we'll be looking at Ab as our starting point)

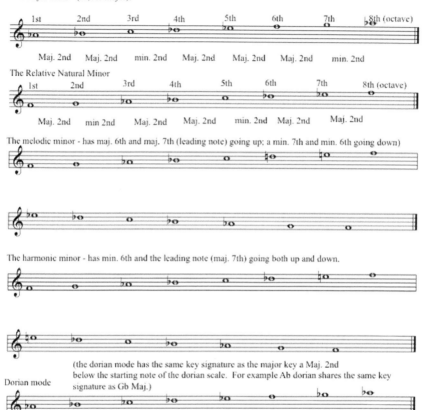

The Major Scale - (so, Ab major):**

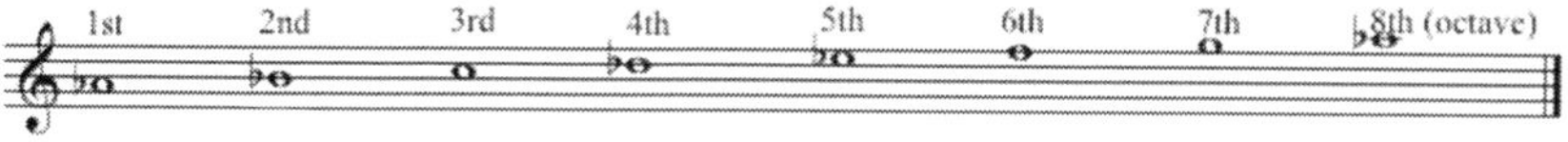

Maj. 2nd Maj. 2nd min. 2nd Maj. 2nd Maj. 2nd Maj. 2nd min. 2nd

The Relative Natural Minor

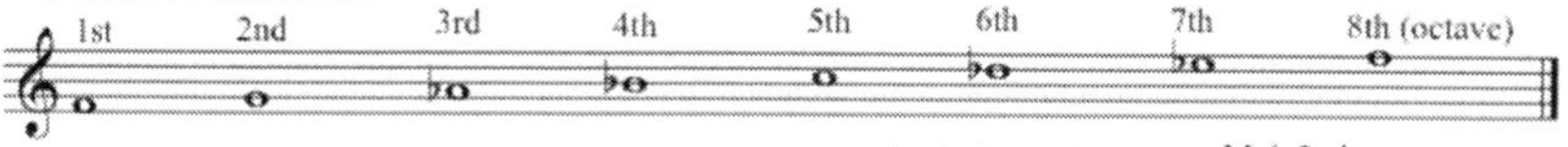

Maj. 2nd min 2nd Maj. 2nd Maj. 2nd min. 2nd Maj. 2nd Maj. 2nd

The melodic minor - has maj. 6th and maj. 7th (leading note) going up; a min. 7th and min. 6th going down)

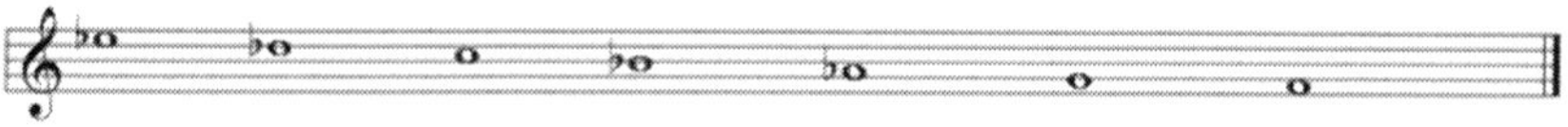

The harmonic minor - has min. 6th and the leading note (maj. 7th) going both up and down.

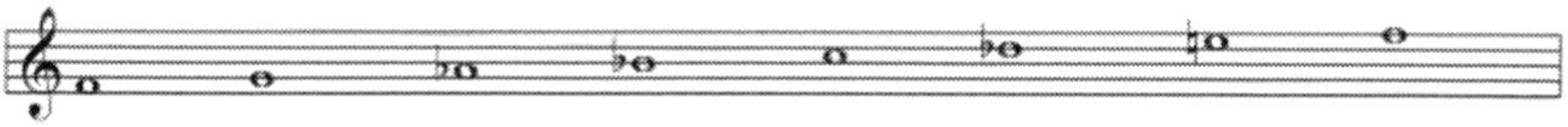

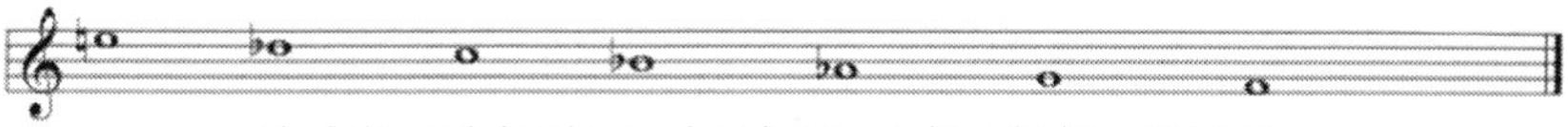

Dorian mode

(the dorian mode has the same key signature as the major key a Maj. 2nd below the starting note of the dorian scale. For example Ab dorian shares the same key signature as Gb Maj.)

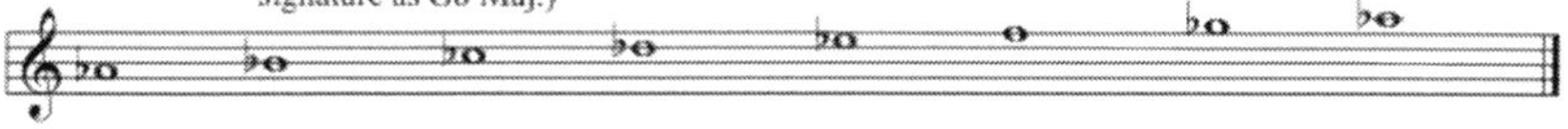

** you can count the intervals in all of these scales in the same way that I have illustrated in the first two scales.

Scales, Modes, Blues

2

Mixolydian Mode (the Mixolydian mode has the same key signature as the major key a Perfect 4th up the starting note of the Mixolydian scale.

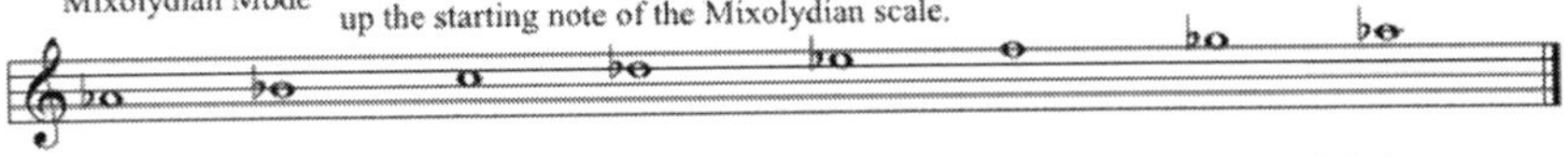

(the Phrygian mode has the same key signature as the major key a Maj. 3rd down from the starting note of the Phrygian scale, in this case, the key of EMaj)

Phrygian

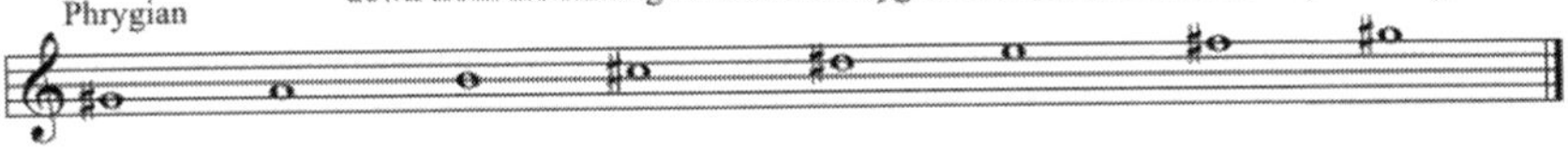

(the Lydian mode has the same key signature as the major key a Perfect 5th up from the starting note of the Lydian scale.

Lydian

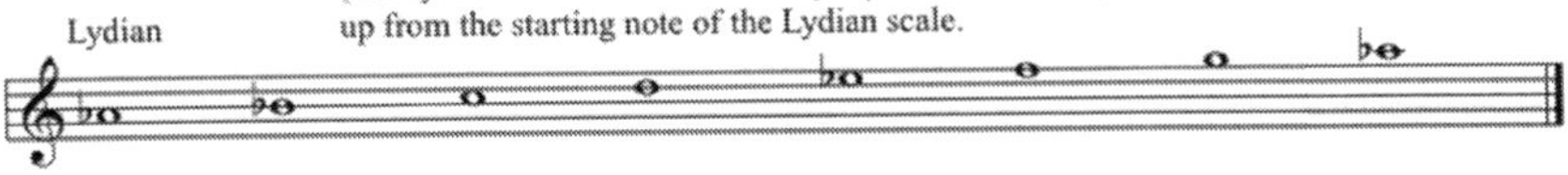

Aeolian (aka: a natural minor scale; same key signature as key 3 half steps above, in this case, B Maj.)

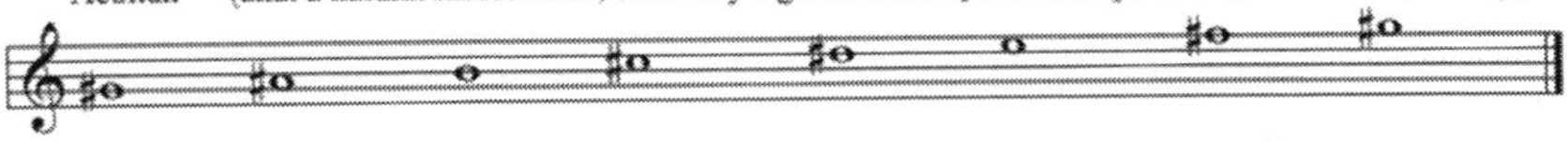

Ionian (aka: Major scale)

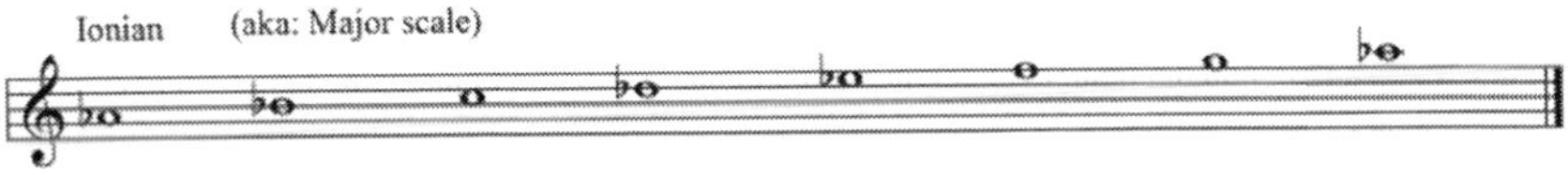

Blues (min. blues)

Blues ("ragtime"/major)

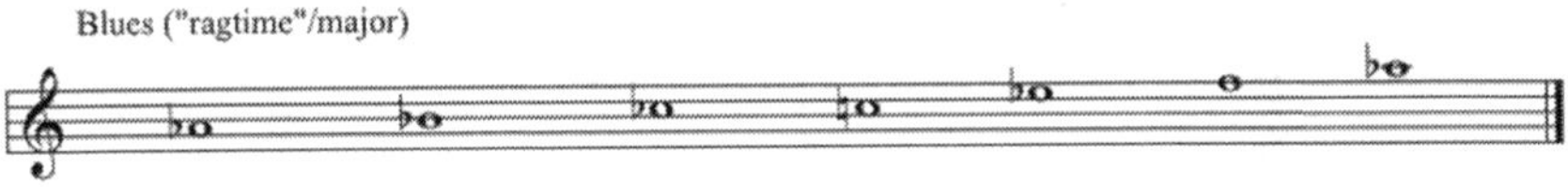

Major, Minor Scales, Modes & Blues

(In these cases, we'll be looking at A as our starting point)

The Major Scale - (so, A major): **

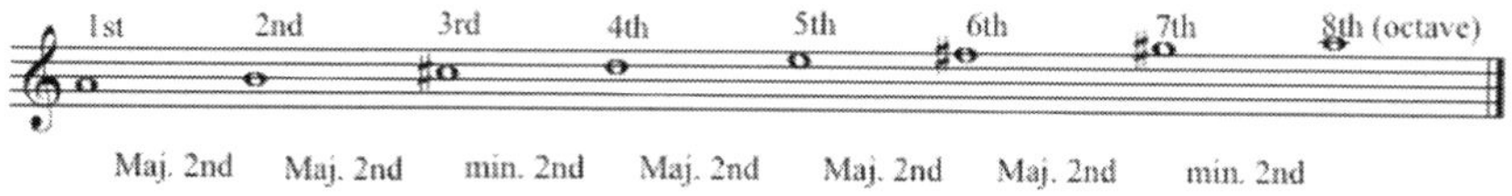

The Relative Natural Minor

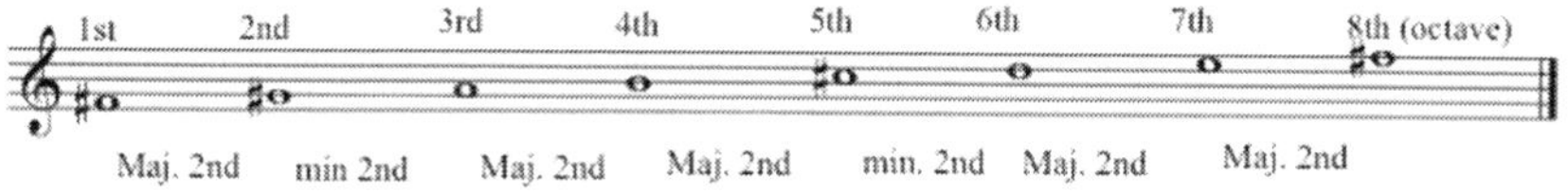

The melodic minor - has maj. 6th and maj. 7th (leading note) going up; a min. 7th and min. 6th going down)

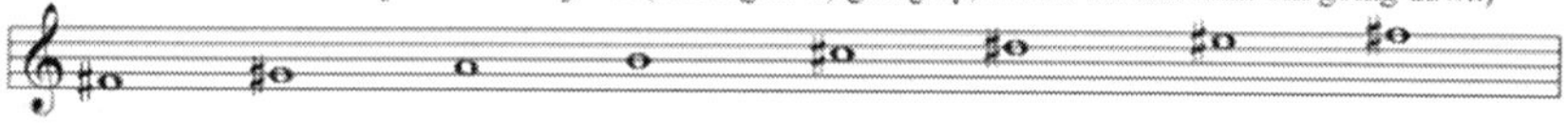

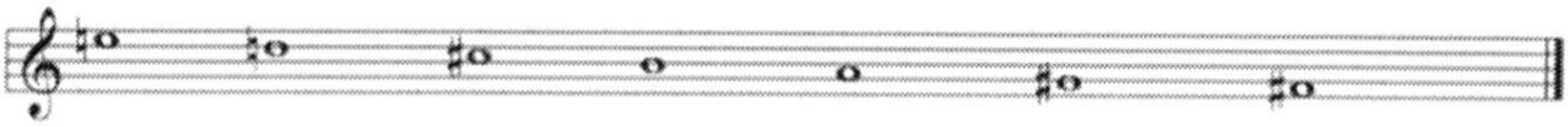

The harmonic minor - has min. 6th and the leading note (maj. 7th) going both up and down.

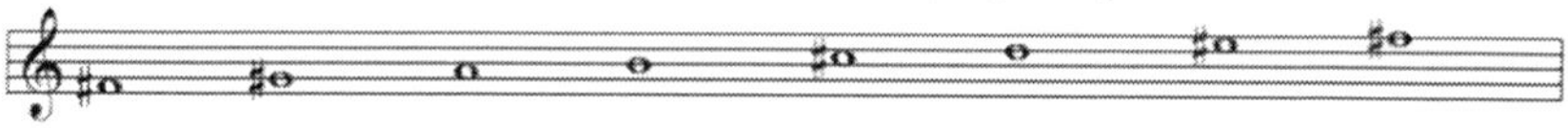

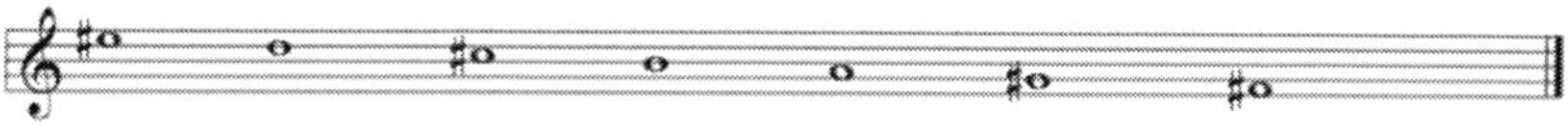

Dorian mode (the dorian mode has the same key signature as the major key a Maj. 2nd below the starting note of the dorian scale. For example A dorian shares the same key signature as G Maj.)

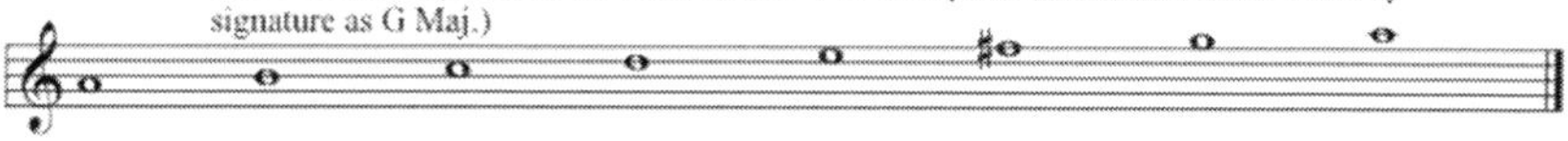

** you can count the intervals in all of these scales in the same way that I have illustrated in the first two scales.

Scales, Modes, Blues

2

Mixolydian Mode (the Mixolydian mode has the same key signature as the major key a Perfect 4th up the starting note of the Mixolydian scale.

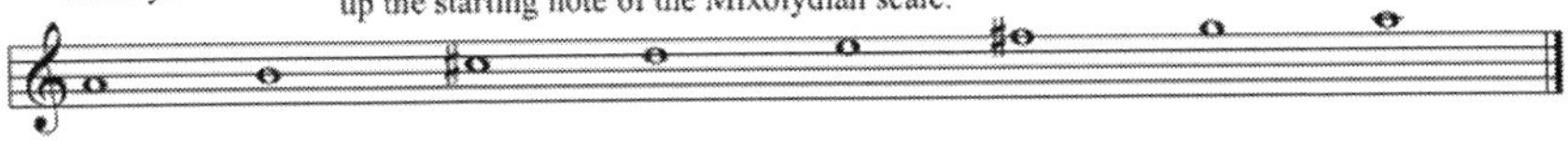

Phrygian (the Phrygian mode has the same key signature as the major key a Maj. 3rd down from the starting note of the Phrygian scale.

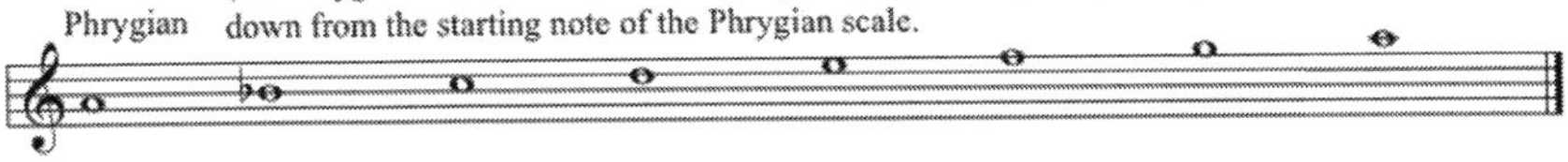

Lydian (the Lydian mode has the same key signature as the major key a Perfect 5th up from the starting note of the Lydian scale.

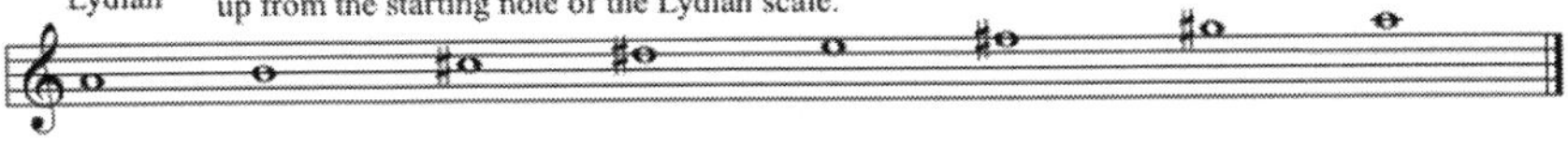

Aeolian (aka: a natural minor scale; same key signature as key 3 half steps above, in this case, C Maj.)

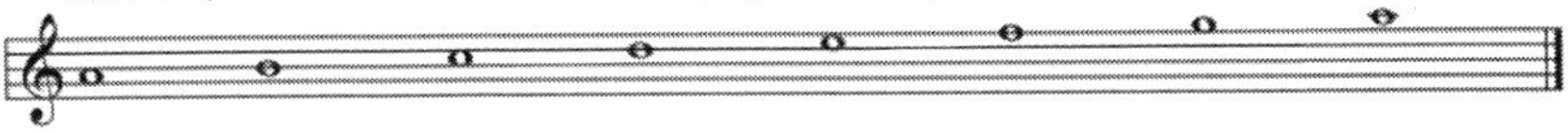

Ionian (aka: Major scale)

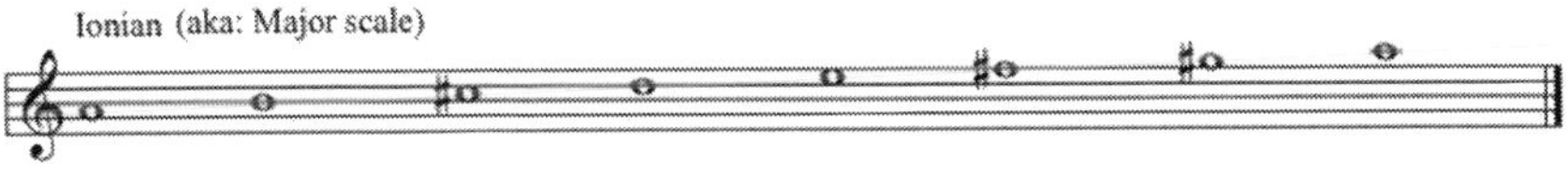

Blues (A min. blues)

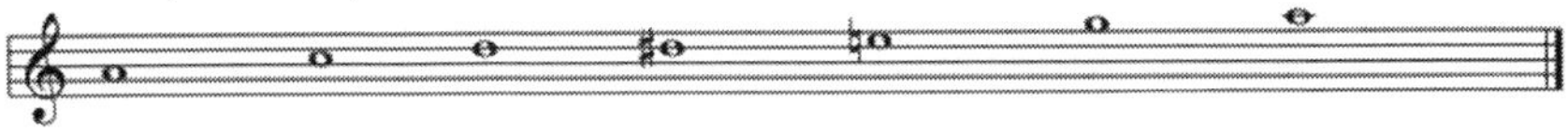

Blues ("ragtime"/major)

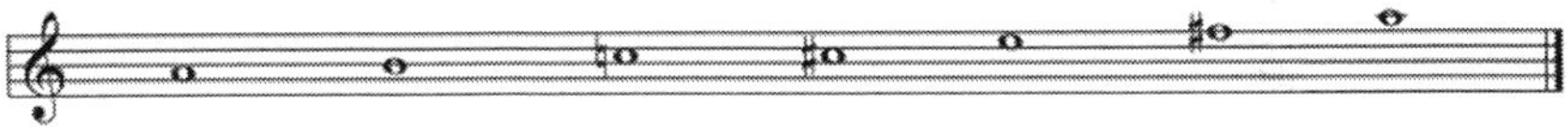

Major, Minor Scales, Modes & Blues

(In these cases, we'll be looking at Bb as our starting point)

The Major Scale - (so, Bb major) **

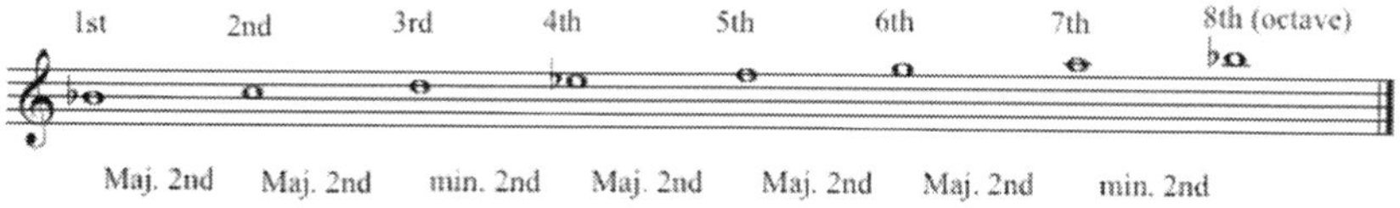

The Relative Natural Minor

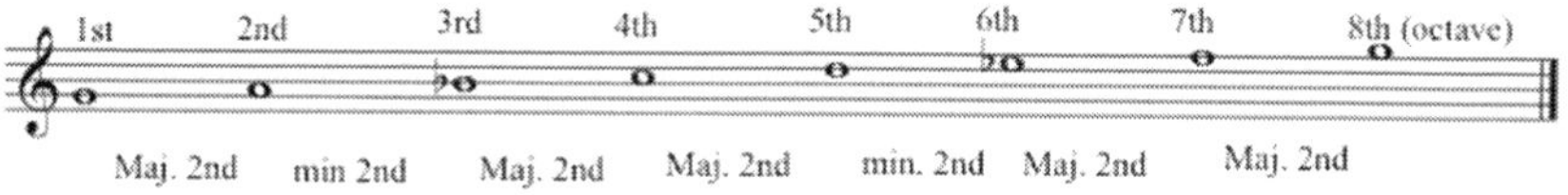

The melodic minor - has maj. 6th and maj. 7th (leading note) going up; a min. 7th and min. 6th going down)

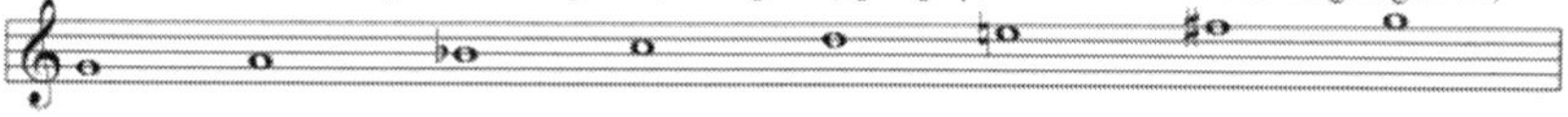

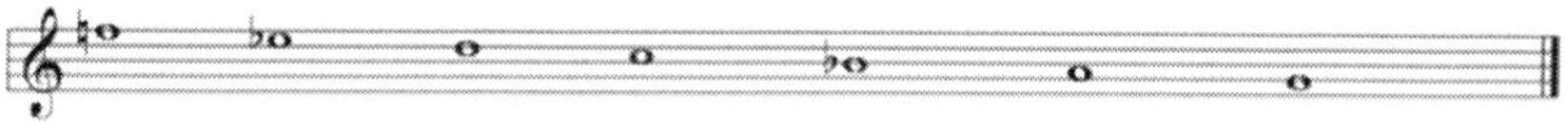

The harmonic minor - has min. 6th and the leading note (maj. 7th) going both up and down.

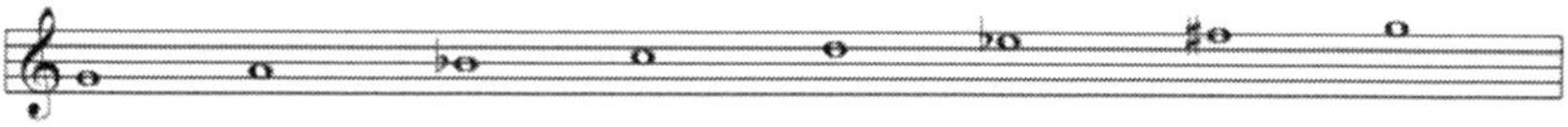

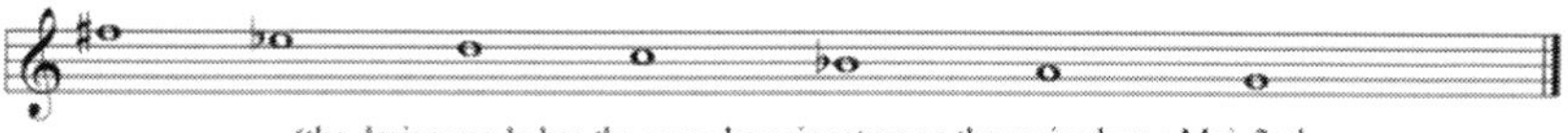

Dorian mode

(the dorian mode has the same key signature as the major key a Maj. 2nd below the starting note of the dorian scale. For example Bb dorian shares the same key signature as Ab Maj.)

** you can count the intervals in all of these scales in the same way that I have illustrated in the first two scales.

Scales, Modes, Blues

2

Mixolydian Mode (the Mixolydian mode has the same key signature as the major key a Perfect 4th up the starting note of the Mixolydian scale.)

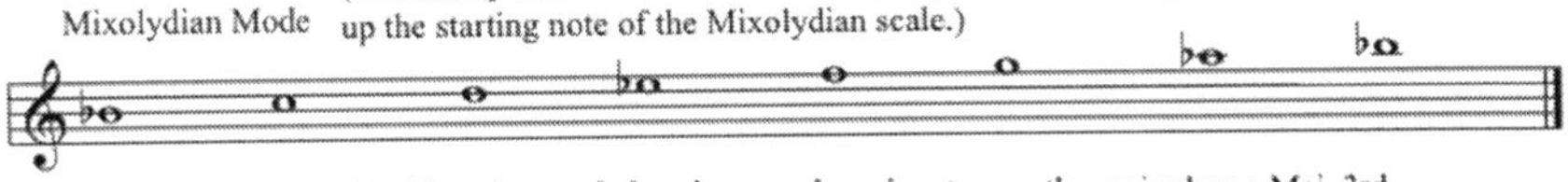

Phrygian (the Phrygian mode has the same key signature as the major key a Maj. 3rd down from the starting note of the Phrygian scale.

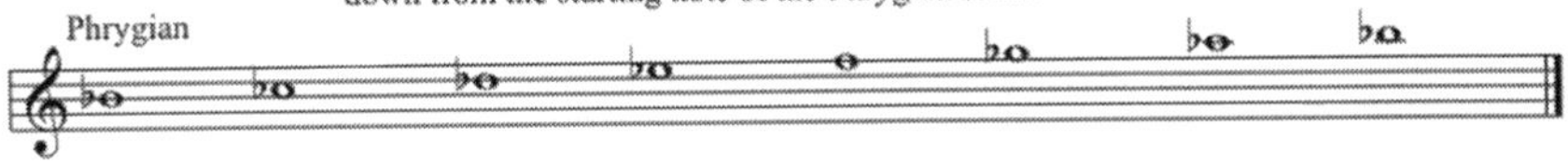

Lydian (the Lydian mode has the same key signature as the major key a Perfect 5th up from the starting note of the Lydian scale.

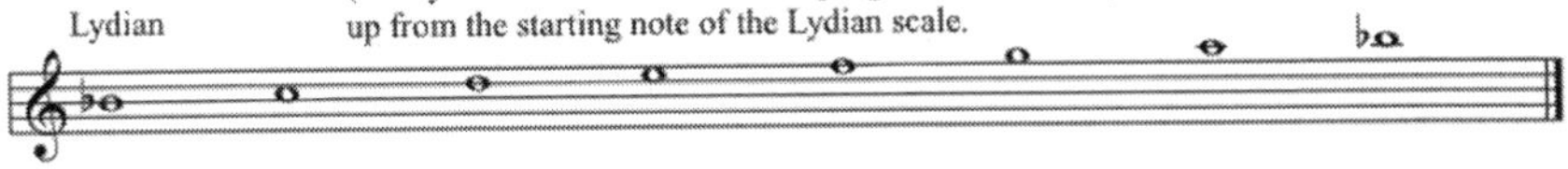

Aeolian (aka: a natural minor scale; same key signature as key 3 half steps above, in this case, Db Maj.)

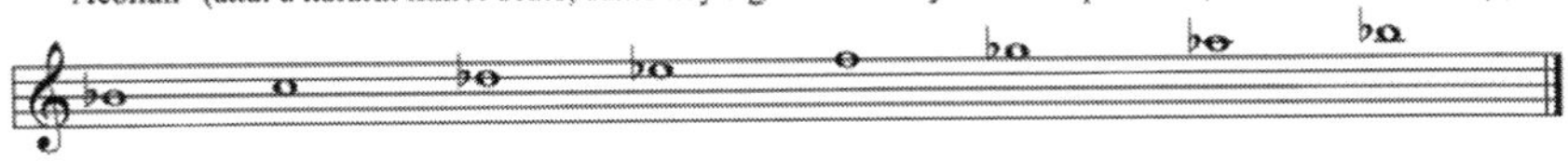

Ionian (aka: Major scale)

Blues (Bb min. blues)

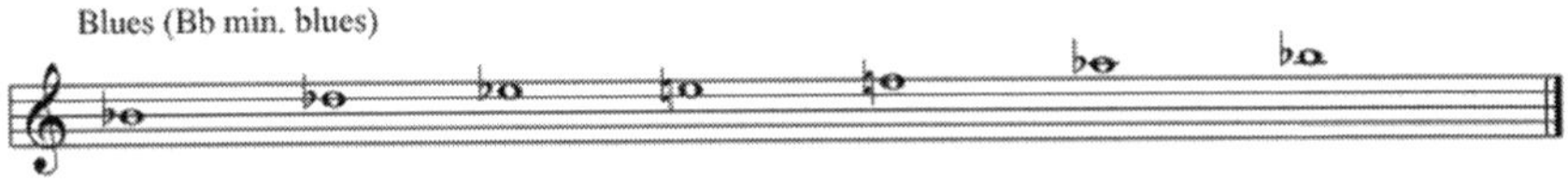

Blues ("ragtime"/major)

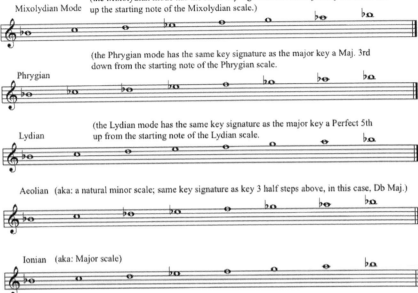

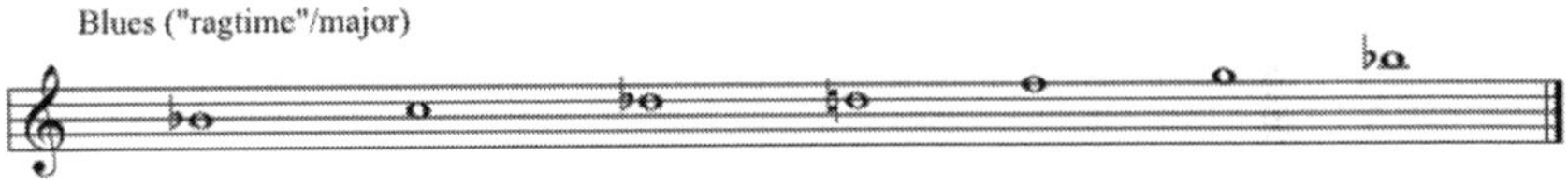

Major, Minor Scales, Modes & Blues

(In these cases, we'll be looking at B as our starting point)

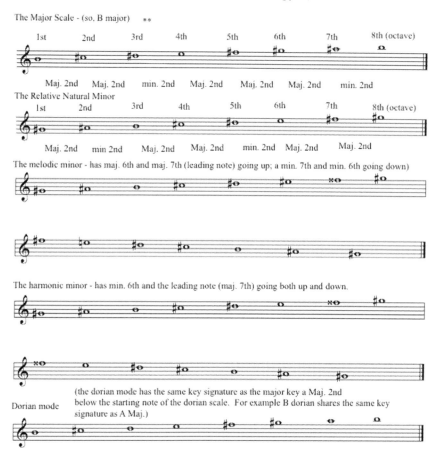

The Major Scale - (so, B major) **

1st 2nd 3rd 4th 5th 6th 7th 8th (octave)

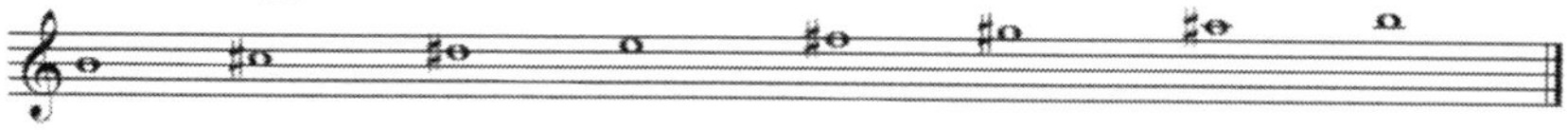

Maj. 2nd Maj. 2nd min. 2nd Maj. 2nd Maj. 2nd Maj. 2nd min. 2nd

The Relative Natural Minor

1st 2nd 3rd 4th 5th 6th 7th 8th (octave)

Maj. 2nd min 2nd Maj. 2nd Maj. 2nd min. 2nd Maj. 2nd Maj. 2nd

The melodic minor - has maj. 6th and maj. 7th (leading note) going up; a min. 7th and min. 6th going down)

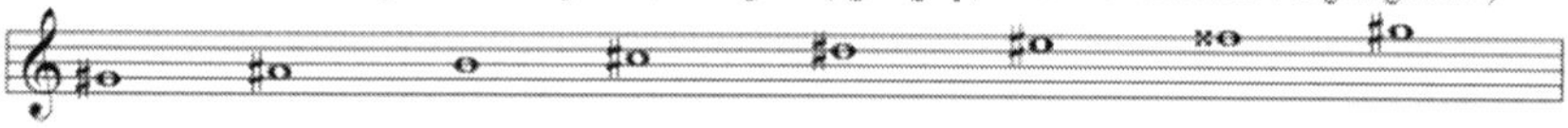

The harmonic minor - has min. 6th and the leading note (maj. 7th) going both up and down.

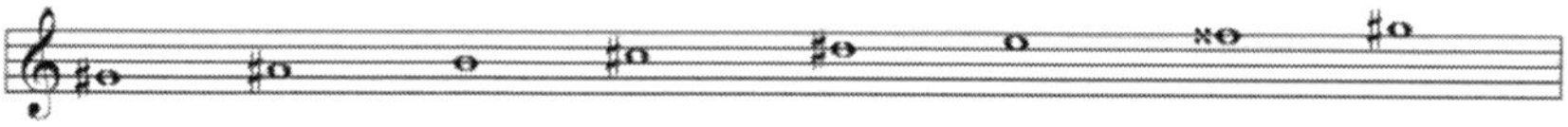

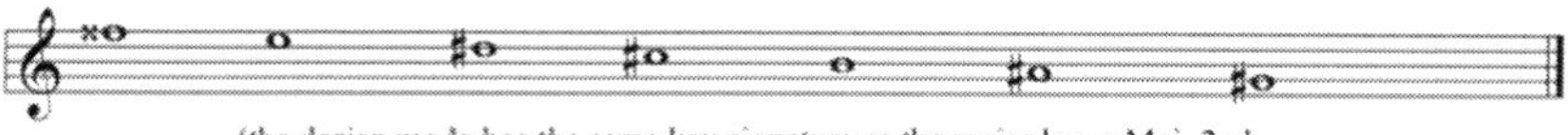

Dorian mode

(the dorian mode has the same key signature as the major key a Maj. 2nd below the starting note of the dorian scale. For example B dorian shares the same key signature as A Maj.)

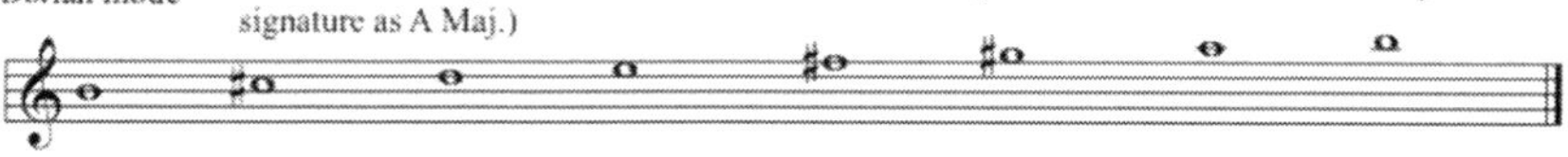

** you can count the intervals in all of these scales in the same way that I have illustrated in the first two scales.

Scales, Modes, Blues

2

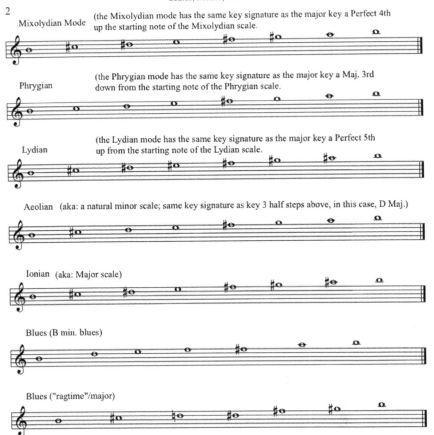

Mixolydian Mode (the Mixolydian mode has the same key signature as the major key a Perfect 4th up the starting note of the Mixolydian scale.

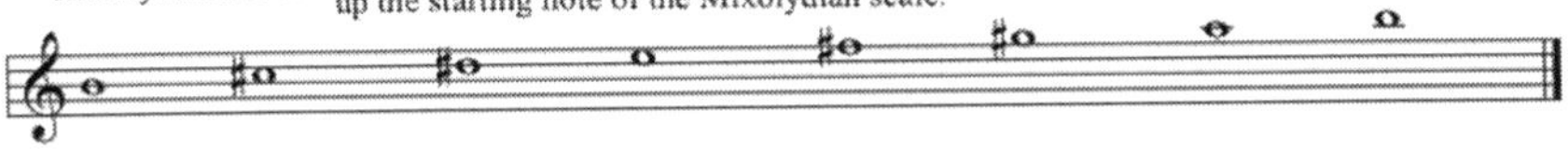

Phrygian (the Phrygian mode has the same key signature as the major key a Maj. 3rd down from the starting note of the Phrygian scale.

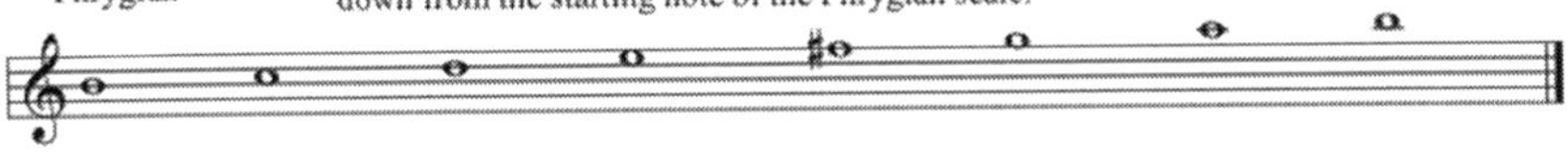

Lydian (the Lydian mode has the same key signature as the major key a Perfect 5th up from the starting note of the Lydian scale.

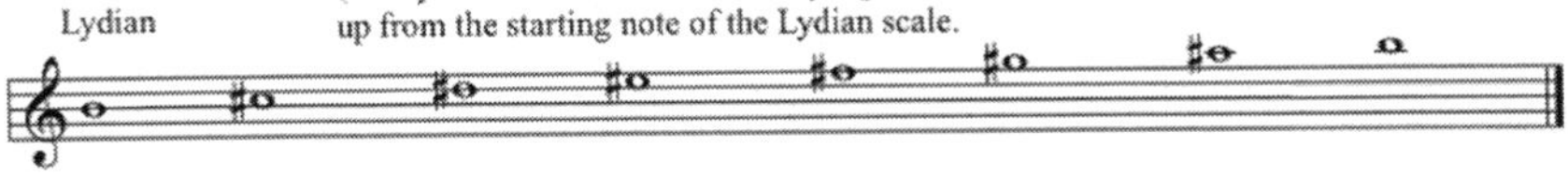

Aeolian (aka: a natural minor scale; same key signature as key 3 half steps above, in this case, D Maj.)

Ionian (aka: Major scale)

Blues (B min. blues)

Blues ("ragtime"/major)

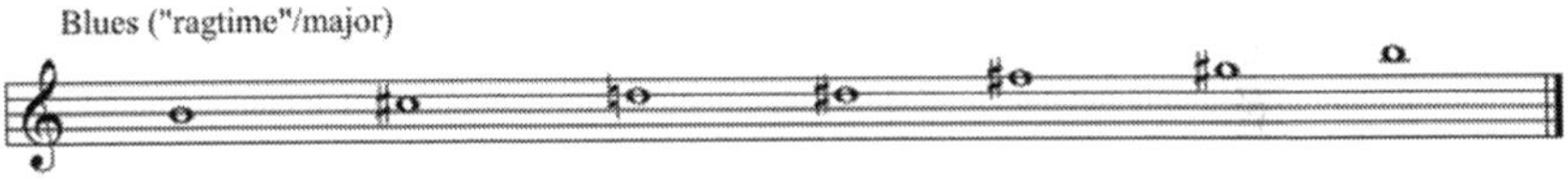

6
RHYTHM

"To live is to be musical, starting with the blood dancing in your veins. Everything living has a rhythm. Do you feel your music?"
—Michael Jackson

"When you sit down and think about what rock 'n' roll music really is, then you have to change that question. Played up-tempo, you call it rock 'n' roll; at a regular tempo, you call it rhythm and blues."
—Little Richard

If you're sitting on your bicycle and you start pedaling, the bike goes forward. Creating rhythm is like pumping the pedals of your music! The rhythmic feel of your song is meaningful—the thing that makes us want to clap, snap, and/or get up and dance! Your rhythms can get us up to go and take us out on the road for a spin!

> Rhythms can be simple and spare or more involved and elaborate. The rhythm is your "groove!" ☺

The feel of your song's rhythm can have various components:

1. When the beats are steady and repeating (aka: the pulse)

2. The momentum of the music (beats per minute)—whether it's fast, or slow—or somewhere in between (aka: the tempo)

> Common approximate beats per minute/tempo ranges for pop songs and comparable classical tempo markings:
>
> 40 to 60-ish (+) beats per minute = ballads (largo/adagio)
>
> 76 to 108-ish (+) beats per minute = medium tempo songs (andante/moderato)
>
> 120-ish (+) beats per minute = dance and techno music (allegro)
>
> 152-ish (+) beats per minute = intense power music! (great for exercise and workouts!) (allegrissimo/presto)

3. The organization of the beats by grouping them into measures of music; the grouping of strong and weak beats (aka: the meter)

Meter

Meter is the organization of music into regularly recurring measures of stressed and unstressed "beats." We do this by using a time signature, bar-lines and the duration of notes.

Example 1

Example 2

Example 3 Example 4

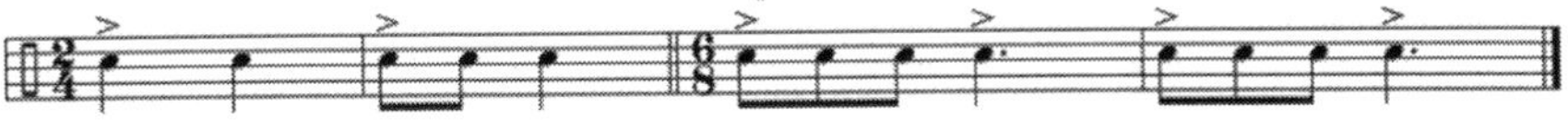

4. You can find the "meter signature" (aka: the time signature) at the beginning of every music piece. It is the two numbers written at the very beginning of the music. The top number indicates how many beats are in each measure. The bottom number indicates which note gets one beat.

Popular times signatures in songwriting:

4/4 (four beats to a bar, quarter note gets one beat)—used frequently

3/4 (three beats to a bar, quarter note gets one beat)

2/4 (two beats to a bar, quarter note gets one beat)

6/8 (six beats to a bar, eighth note gets one beat)

Time Signatures

> The length that a note is held is the note's duration. A whole note is equal to two half notes. A half note is equal to two quarter notes. A quarter note is equal to two eight notes, and an eighth note is equal to two sixteenth notes, and so on.

5. When we count note values smaller than the beat (aka: the subdivision of rhythms, or subdivision), we are separating the meter into shorter beat parts or components.

Subdivision & Counting

It's possible to divide a 4/4 bar of music in different ways to create various results.

To hear how changes in subdividing can create completely different kinds of music, take a listen to:

a. Rock and Pop music: for an 8th note feel

b. Disco Dance songs: for a straight and steady quarter note feel

c. Reggae, Funk, and R & B music: for a 16th note feel

d. Rap and Hip Hop: for a 16th swing feel

e. Blues, some 40's and 50's tunes, and Bebop: for a triplet feel (groupings of three notes per beat)

Exercise:

1. Listen to a few songs on your list of favorite songs. What kinds of rhythms do you hear?
2. With rhythm specifically in mind, listen to some recordings of Bob Marley, Madonna, Led Zeppelin, Dolly Parton, Santana, Eminem, Prince, Adele, Taylor Swift, Elvis Presley, and The Village People.
3. Compare and contrast.

6. The clarity of your music: might be thin, thick, light, or heavy—or somewhere in between. The character of your song can be influenced by how much you've got going on in your rhythms.

Here is an example of thinner rhythmic lines compared with more active lines:

7. When the rhythmic emphasis shifts to the weak beats instead of the strong beats (aka: syncopation), it can give the music momentum.

Syncopation

Examples of Syncopation:

EXERCISE:

1. Put together a rhythmic idea on any one chord.
2. Play around with the feel, the rhythmic idea, and the tempo.

EXERCISE:

1. Take the rhythmic feel from a song you love.
2. Create a brand new chord progression of your own.

EXERCISE:

1. Take the rhythmic idea (motive) from a song you like.
2. Choose a different chord progression from another song you like.
3. Combine them.
4. Invent your own melody over this chord progression and rhythm. See if this melody suggests any lyric ideas to you.

Or:

5. You can also reverse this last process by looking through your notebook/journal to find a lyric idea. See if that lyric suggests a melody for your new rhythmic chord progression.

EXERCISE:

1. Use one or two chords, and write three different rhythms for four bars:
    a. Use quarter notes, half notes, and whole notes
    b. Use quarter notes and eighth notes
    c. Use sixteenth notes and eighth notes

Rhythmic Exercise Examples

A.

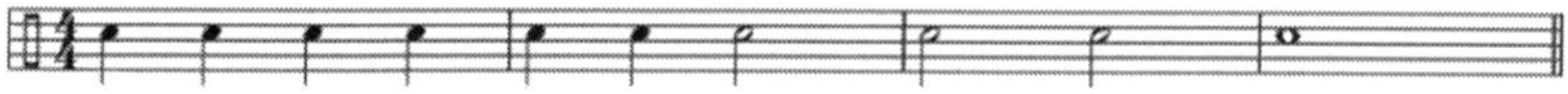

B.

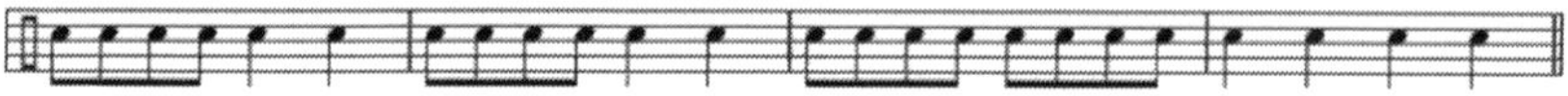

C.

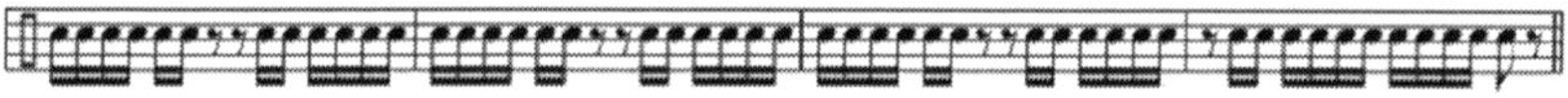

EXERCISE:

1. Construct rhythmic sections for a song by creating an eight-bar verse and an eight-bar chorus with contrasting rhythms to distinguish the verse from the chorus.
2. Use repetition, variation, and combine different motives.

Sample Rhythms For Verse & Chorus Using Repetition & Variation

VERSE - uses repetition

A

CHORUS - uses variation in the last bar

B

You can also experiment by combining two different motives within your sections.

Combining Two Different Rhythmic Motives

EXERCISE:

Listen to a few favorite songs and see how the different sections vary rhythmically. See if you can break them down and analyze them for your own inspiration.

7
CREATIVITY

"Songwriting is a kind of therapy for both the writer and the listener if you choose to use it that way. When you see that stuff help other people that's great and wonderful confirmation that you're doing the right thing."
—Sting

"A lot of times songs are very much of a moment, that you just encapsulate. They come to you, you write them, you feel good that day, or bad that day."
—Mick Jagger

What is creativity?

- Creativity is the capacity to create!
- It is the ability to manifest something out of nothing with the use of your own imagination and skill.

As members of the human species, we all possess basic needs (air, water, food, love—to name a few universal needs!) In this regard, we are all universally the same.

That being said, we are also all unique and original—like snowflakes! There is no one snowflake that is exactly the same as another snowflake. This makes it both challenging and rewarding to create songs that can be understood on a universal level—and yet be brand new, not just "copy cats" of something that's already been said or done.

If we can strive to express our original take on things with our own unique perspectives and emotions—we can move people, help people, and even help ourselves all at the same time. This is a pretty amazing and exciting aspect of creativity.

In order to be creative, we have to make room for it to happen. Creativity takes practice.

How can we encourage creativity in our lives?

Here are some ways to make it happen:

1. To practice consistently, it helps to make a habit of it.
2. To make being creative a habit, it helps to make time for it.
3. To make time for it, it helps to pick a certain time or map out specific times that you can commit to regularly.

To make a commitment to creativity, you can pick the same time every day, or pick a few regular times every week—whatever works for your schedule.

EXERCISE:

1. Take a walk (and if you have a dog, you can take your dog on a walk with you!)
2. Let your mind wander.
3. Notice what thoughts are coming to you in this relaxed state. What are you thinking about?
4. Do you notice birds? Listen...Do you see houses, trees, kids in the neighborhood? Take a look around...
5. See if there's a story or a feeling that would lend itself to a new song idea.

The previous exercise will also work with:

1. Brushing your teeth
2. Sitting in a chair (at the library?)
3. Bike riding
4. Skateboarding
5. Sitting on a bench (in the park? at the mall?)
6. Washing your hair
7. Petting and/or feeding your: cat, dog, guinea pig, rabbit
8. Unloading (or loading!) the dishwasher
9. Falling asleep at night

10. Waking up in the morning (while still lying in bed awhile)

11. Walking around a museum

12. Walking around a park

13. Folding laundry

14. Gardening

15. Watering plants or the lawn

16. Washing a car

17. Making a bed

18. Getting dressed

19. Taking a bath

20. Riding around in a car and looking out the window (while someone else is driving!)

21. Looking up at the stars at night

22. Watching the clouds move around in the sky

It will be helpful to have a little notebook near you to jot things down when you're inspired. Many of these ideas work best when you're by yourself, without a lot of other conversation going on to distract you.

Sometimes listening or observing what other people are saying and doing can be inspirational. So, I want to add:

23. Listening to conversations.

Having said that, do this with a grain of salt! I don't want to advocate being rude or invading other people's privacy. It's more of a suggestion to keep your ears open for little snippets or nuggets of conversation that inspire you in ways you might not have been open to before.

Even a single word (or two) can turn your mind on to new ideas for creative use.

8

ANATOMY OF A SONG

"The key to longevity is to learn every aspect of music that you can."
—Prince

"Out of my entire annual output of songs, perhaps two, or at the most three, came as a result of inspiration. We can never rely on inspiration. When we most want it, it does not come."
—George Gershwin

In this chapter, I show you some of my "journalings," scribbles, ideas, notes—the predecessors to the final lyrics of some of my songs. I hope these scribbles and notes will encourage you to be as free and as "messy" and as nonjudgmental as you need to be in order to get things down on paper—and in order to get yourself going. You can always edit and perfect things later.

After the initial scribbles, I include copies of these same scribblings as they morph into more (almost like) "poetry-ish" lines, and then become rough lyrics. You can also see where I keep track of the number of syllables I'm using for each lyric line so that I can keep everything consistent in each section.

Then finally, I include the lyrics to the completed songs so that you can see where they came from.

I want to encourage you to keep all of your extractions, all the things you've "thrown out."

- Look at all of your second choices because you never know!
- Save your scribbles!

I save my scribbles and rough drafts because they might lead me to something else that's golden. They might put me on another track that ends up being a really good song. Then again...maybe not! But that's okay too.

> Be open to stumbling upon a piece of gold.

At times I find that my lyric writes itself backward. It's almost like a puzzle. I know where I'm trying to get to (the end of the story), and then it's a matter of working my way to the end I have in mind. I might end up somewhere else, but my initial "plan" somehow got me going.

I write out the ideas, and then I shape the ideas into patterns and rhymes. I try to make the rhymes as interesting as I can.

Sometimes, I begin with a title idea and make a list of ideas that go with the title and/or lists of possible rhymes. I might start making a list of everything I can think about that has to do with my song idea and take it from there, or hold onto the list for later.

How do you find the music in the lyrics? Many times, you can look and see that:

1. The words already somehow encourage music.
2. The words introduce a certain feeling or atmosphere that inspires music.
3. The words have sound and rhythm to them.

The following are three examples of initial ramblings that lead ultimately to my final lyrics for these three songs:

1. "Love Is the Journey"
2. "Every Living Thing Must Go"
3. "Not Being Joni Mitchell"

First song: "Love Is the Journey" (The italics are from my original notes)

Idea: write something about how a single relationship that lasts for years can be like taking a huge journey across uncharted seas; territories of the unknown; almost like being an explorer, always meeting this person as if for the first time, over and over again. Do we really ever know someone? It's like sailing off into the unknown. . .Love is the ultimate journey and the real adventure.

idea:
Sailing off into the unknown

(X) The journey

Beginnings are the easy things
roses, ~~sweets~~ kisses, ~~&~~ diamond rings
What kind of music do you like
~~Dancing~~ Holding each other through the night
~~Do you love me? Maybe so~~ Dancing close, ~~holding hands~~
~~Overthinking makes my~~ the heart flutters
~~Not so certain where we stand~~

Beginnings ~~are~~ ios the easy things
flirty email, roses, kisses, ~~diamond rings~~ cell phone rings
~~Not so certain where we stand~~
~~Dancing close & holding hands~~
~~Do Are you free to~~ do
What kind of music ~~do you~~ do we like
Do ~~you~~ we want to stay tonight?
Dancing close & holding hands
Not so certain where we stand —,
~~Feeling like a triumph~~

Take a trip & stay for years
Where is that love I used to know
Is it gone or did it grow

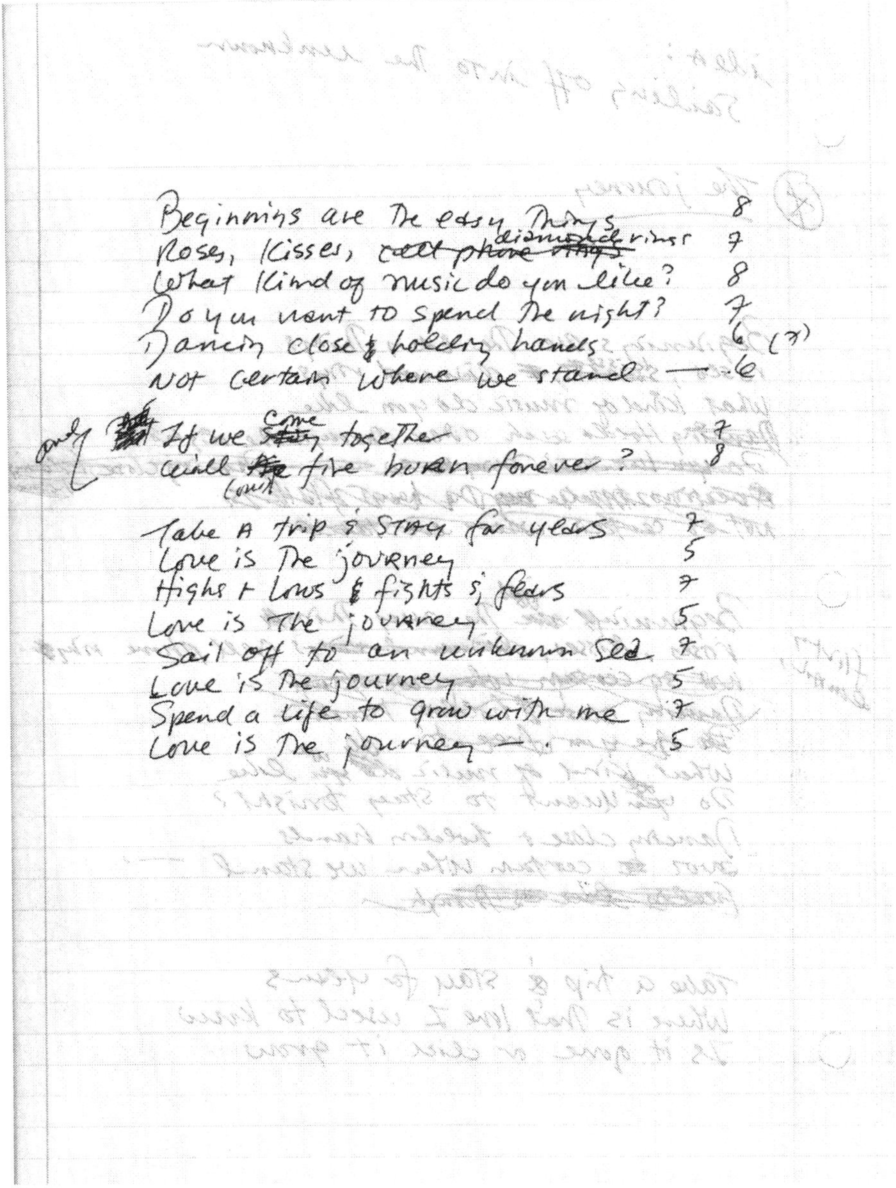

Beginnings are the easy things 8
Roses, kisses, ~~cell phone rings~~ diamond rings 7
What kind of music do you like? 8
Do you want to spend the night? 7
Dancing close & holding hands 6 (7)
Not certain where we stand — 6

only If we ~~stay~~ come together 7
Will ~~the~~ could fire burn forever? 8

Take a trip & stay for years 7
Love is the journey 5
Highs + lows & fights & fears 7
Love is the journey 5
Sail off to an unknown sea 7
Love is the journey 5
Spend a life to grow with me 7
Love is the journey —. 5

To look at you I see myself 8
Thru the sickness thru the health 7
The Heart beats like a daily prayer 8
& Every morning you are there 7
~~A different love is in the~~ past (8)
~~If~~ our young love's ~~in the past?~~ Those ~~early~~ days live in the past
~~A different time is in our past~~ ? Each day we make them
 last
~~Cause we stay~~ together
~~One~~ ~~the fire burn~~ forever ~~&~~
'cause we Belong together
~~keep the~~ fire burn forever
to make our

~~The journey is true~~
take a trip & stay for years
~~where~~ Love is the Journey
~~take this life &~~ ~~feel your fears~~
~~Take this~~ Love & Hate, fights &
Try to understand ~~our~~ fears
Cause Love is the journey
Sail off to an unknown sea
where ~~there~~ Love is the journey
~~Take the time~~
Spend a life to grow with no nye ~~in the past~~
Love is the journey.

~~There is no~~ A promise is no
~~guarantee~~ garantee

Those early days live in the past
~~If our young~~ ~~love is in the past~~
~~Each~~ we make them
Each day we make them
past

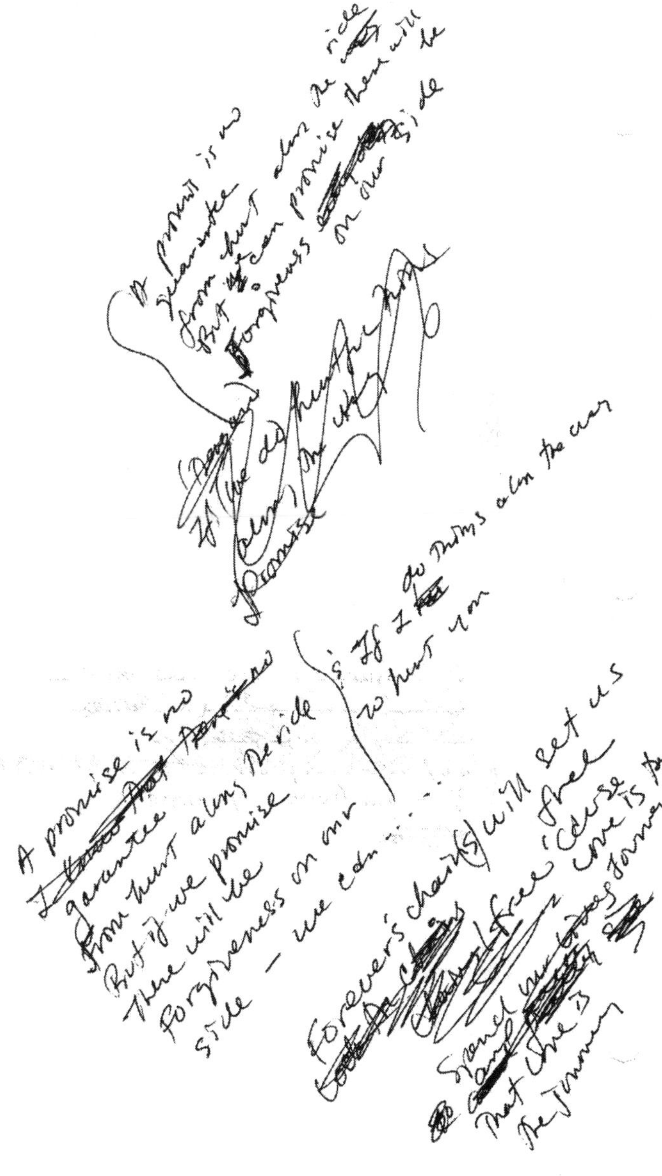
A promise is no
guarantee
from hurt along the ride
But if we can promise there will be
forgiveness on our side
If I do things along the way
to hurt you
A promise is no
guarantee
from hurt along the ride
But if we promise
there will be
forgiveness on our
side — we can
Forever's chains will set us
free
Love is the journey

Love Is The Journey

Beginnings are the easy things
Roses, kisses, diamond rings
What kind of music do you like?
Do we want to spend the night?
Dancing close & holding hands
Not certain where we stand —.

But if we come together
How will the fire burn forever ?

Chorus:

Take a trip & stay for years
Love is the journey
Highs & lows & fights & fears
Love is the journey
Sail off to an unknown sea
Love is the journey
Spend a life to grow w/ me (2x: Spend your life, grow old w/ me)
Love is the journey.

To look at you I see myself
Through the sickness through the health
my ~~The~~ heart beats like a daily prayer
Every morning you are there
Those early days live in the past
Eden night we make them last —.

'Cause we belong together
(To) ~~Let's make~~ ~~the~~ fire burn forever —.
(com)

Love Is the Journey

Beginnings are the easy things
Roses, kisses, diamond rings
What kind of music do you like?
Are we going to spend the night,
Dancing close and holding hands?
Not certain where we stand—

But if we come together
How will the fire burn forever?

Chorus:

Take a trip and stay for years
Love is the journey
Highs and lows and fights and fears
Love is the journey
Sail off to an unknown sea
Spend a life to grow with me—cause love,
Love is the journey

To look at you I see myself
Through the sickness, through the health
My heart beats like a daily prayer
Every morning you are there
Those early days live in the past
Each night we make them last—

'Cause we belong together
Letting our fire burn forever

Chorus:

Take a trip and stay for years
Love is the journey
Highs and lows and fights and fears
Love is the journey
Sail off to an unknown sea
Spend your life, grow old with me—and love,
Love is the journey

Bridge:

A promise is no guarantee
        from hurt along the ride
But if we promise there will be
        forgiveness on our side—we can—

Chorus:

Take a trip and stay for years
Love is the journey
Highs and lows and fights and fears
Love is the journey
Sail off to an unknown sea
Forever's chains will set us free—where love,
Love is the journey—our love,
Love is the journey.

Second song: "Every Living Thing Must Go" (The italics are from my original notes)

Idea: write something about time, and the illusion of time; how we all are here and then, gone. Yet...somehow forever. The idea of being here "now" or the past or future: a fiction; we have no concept of time. Life/death/eternity.

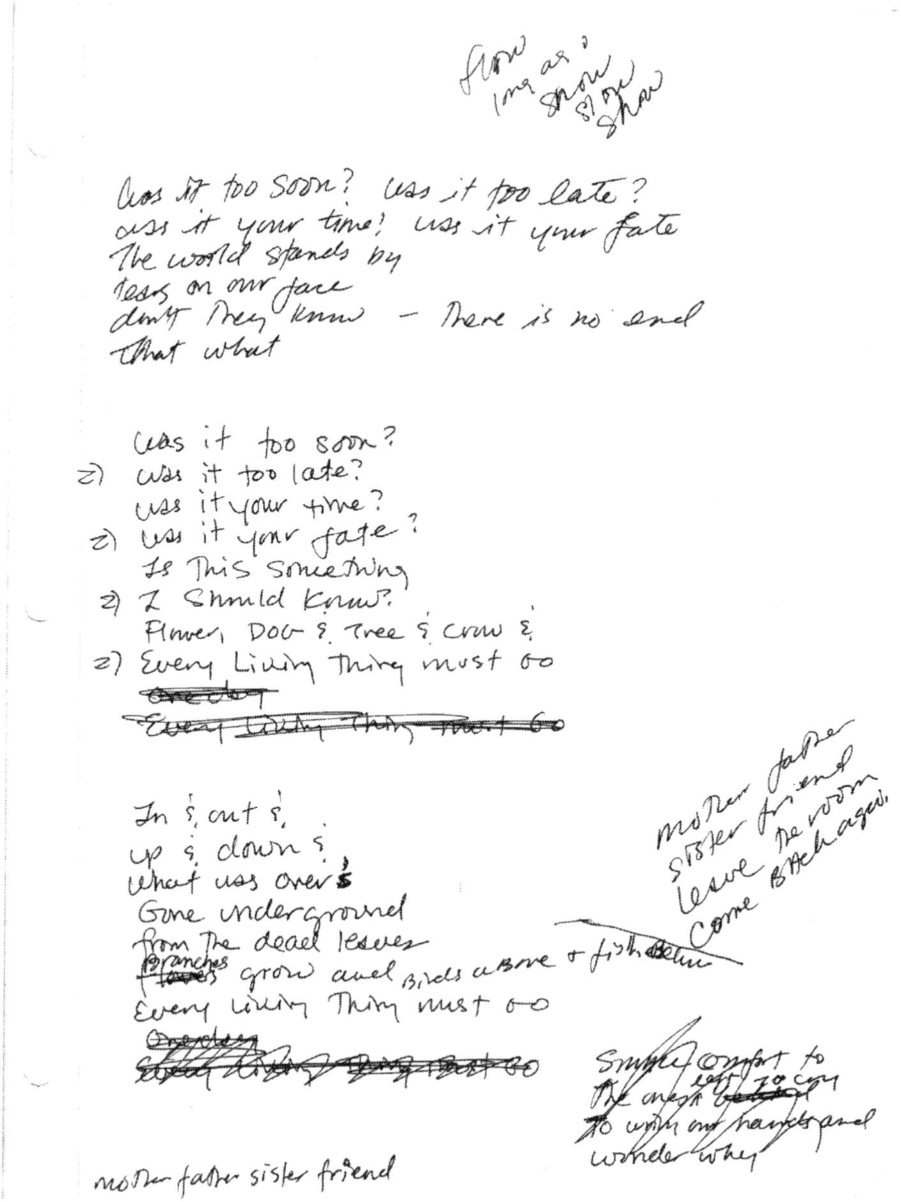

flow
long as
snow
slow
show

Was it too soon? Was it too late?
Was it your time! Was it your fate
The world stands by
tears on our face
don't they know — there is no end
that what

Was it too soon?
2) Was it too late?
Was it your time?
2) Was it your fate?
Is this something
2) I should know?
Flower, Dog & Tree & Crow &
2) Every Living Thing must Go
~~One day~~
~~Every Living Thing must Go~~

In & out &
up & down &
What was over's
Gone underground
from the dead leaves
~~Leaves~~ Branches grow and Birds above & fish ~~Below~~
Every Living Thing must Go
~~One day~~
~~Every Living Thing must Go~~

mother father
sister friend
leave the room
Come Back again

Simple comfort to
The ~~eye~~ empty ~~[illegible]~~ to cry
To wipe our hands and
wonder why

mother father sister friend

was it too soon 4
was it too late 4
was it your time 4
was it your fate 4
was it something ~~[illegible]~~ ~~is~~ was this something 4
~~you wanted me to know~~ I'm suppose to know? I should know?
~~wait for~~

Flower, dog, tree, ~~and~~ crow 5 6
~~Dog or cat, tree or crow~~
Every living thing must go
one day
Every living thing must go

In, out, up, down
~~of~~ over, under
& above ~~the ground~~ ground
sinking

In & out &
up & down &
now ~~was~~ over
lives ~~started~~ underground

Begin and End
Above and Below ~~[illegible]~~
Every~~thing~~ Living thing must Go
one day
Every Living thing must go

mother father sister friend
All left behind to cry
~~[illegible]~~
forgetting that there is no end

fish ~~with~~ fly above
birds swim below
Start the middle
At the end
Finish up ~~to~~ &
Begin again

Every Living Thing

Was it too soon?
Was it too late?
Was it your time?
Was it your fate?
Is this something
I should know —
flower, dog & tree & crow &
Every Living Thing must Go —.

In & out &
up & down &
What was over's
Gone under ground
From the dead leaves
Branches grow
Birds above & fish below &
Every Living thing must Go —.

Whisper to me
Inside my dreams
I will be listening to all you say
You are the wind
That blows through the trees
To tell me you're waiting to meet me someday —.

Mother Father
Sister friend
Leave the room
Come back again
The future is
So long ago
Summer comes
To Bring The Snow (where)
Every Living Thing must Go —.

Every Living Thing Must Go

Was it too soon?
Was it too late?
Was it your time?
Was it your fate?
Is this something
I should know?
Flower, dog and bee and crow and
Every living thing must go.

In and out and
Up and down
What's over has
Gone under ground
From the dead leaves
Branches grow
Birds above and fish below and
Every living thing must go.

Whisper to me
Inside my dreams
I will be listening to all that you say
You are the wind
That blows through the trees
To tell me you're waiting to meet me someday

Mother Father
Sister Friend
We leave the room
Come back again
The future is
So long ago
Summer comes to bring the snow and

Every living thing must go.
Every living thing must go.

Every Living Thing Must Go © by Lisa Donovan Lukas
MUST WRITE MUSIC (ASCAP)

> Third song: "Not Being Joni Mitchell" (The italics are from my original notes)
>
> *Idea: write something about "expectations"—how I thought my life should be (like Joni Mitchell's life) and how it's turned out—song about letting go of expectations so you can cherish what your life* ***is****—and let it become what it's* ***suppose*** *to be. Hang out in gratitude for what you* ***are****.*

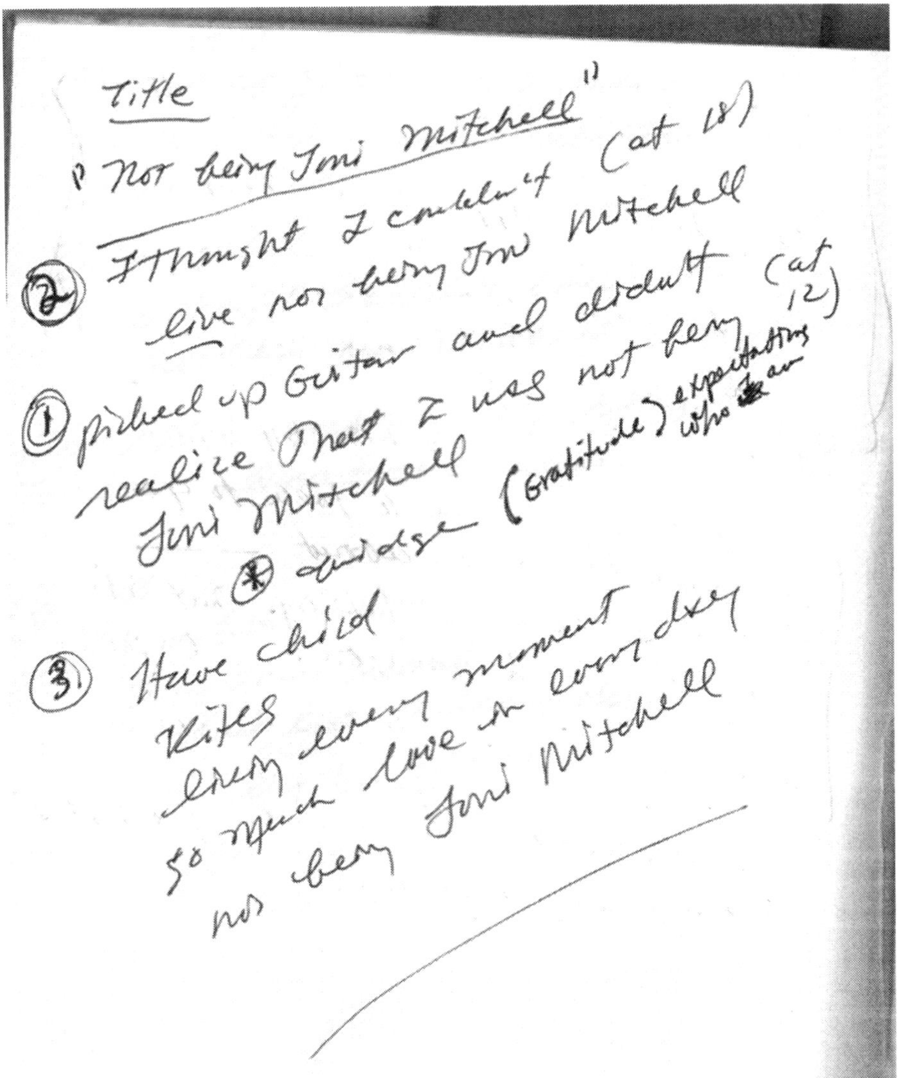

Title

"Not being Joni Mitchell"

② I thought I couldn't (at 18)
live not being Joni Mitchell

① picked up Guitar and didn't (at 12)
realize that I was not being
Joni Mitchell

* bridge (Gratitude) expectations who I am

③ Have child
Kites
living every moment
So much love in every day
not being Joni Mitchell

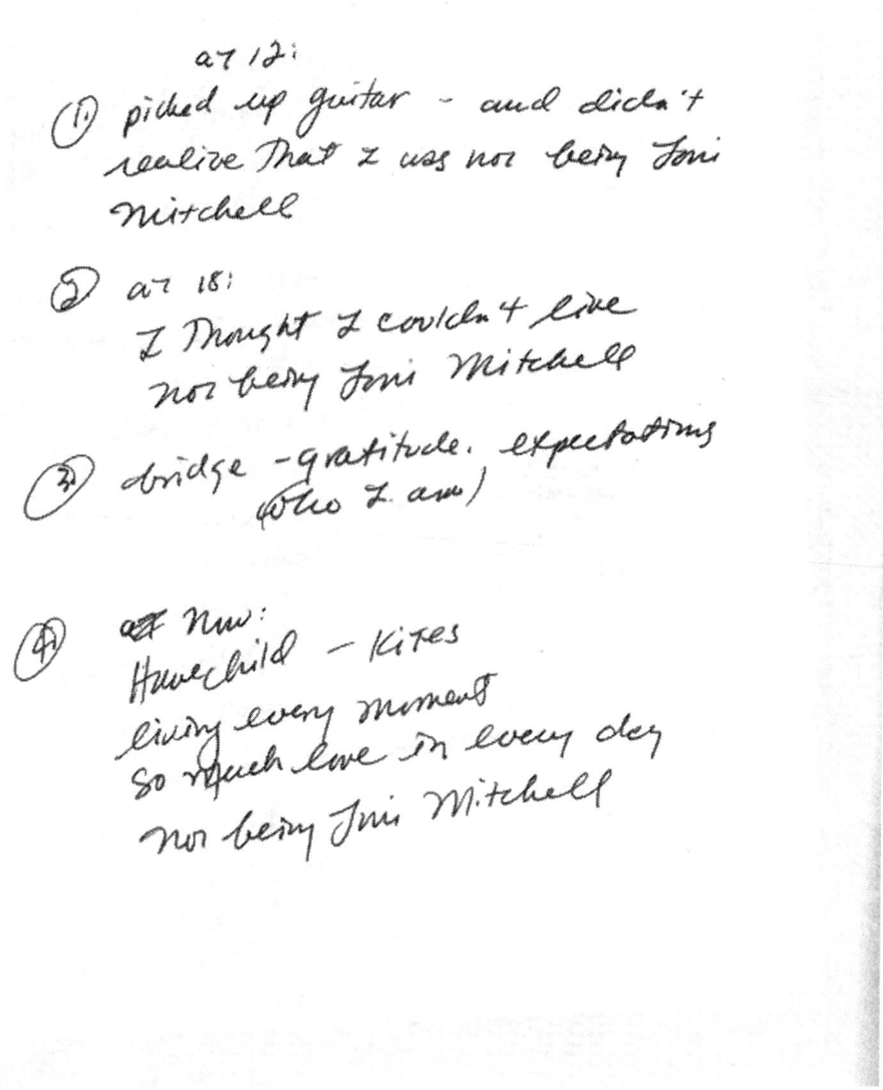

at 12:
(1) picked up guitar - and didn't realize that I was not being Joni Mitchell

(2) at 18:
I thought I couldn't live not being Joni Mitchell

(3) bridge - gratitude. expectations
(who I am)

(4) ~~at~~ now:
Have child - kites
living every moment
so much love in every day
not being Joni Mitchell

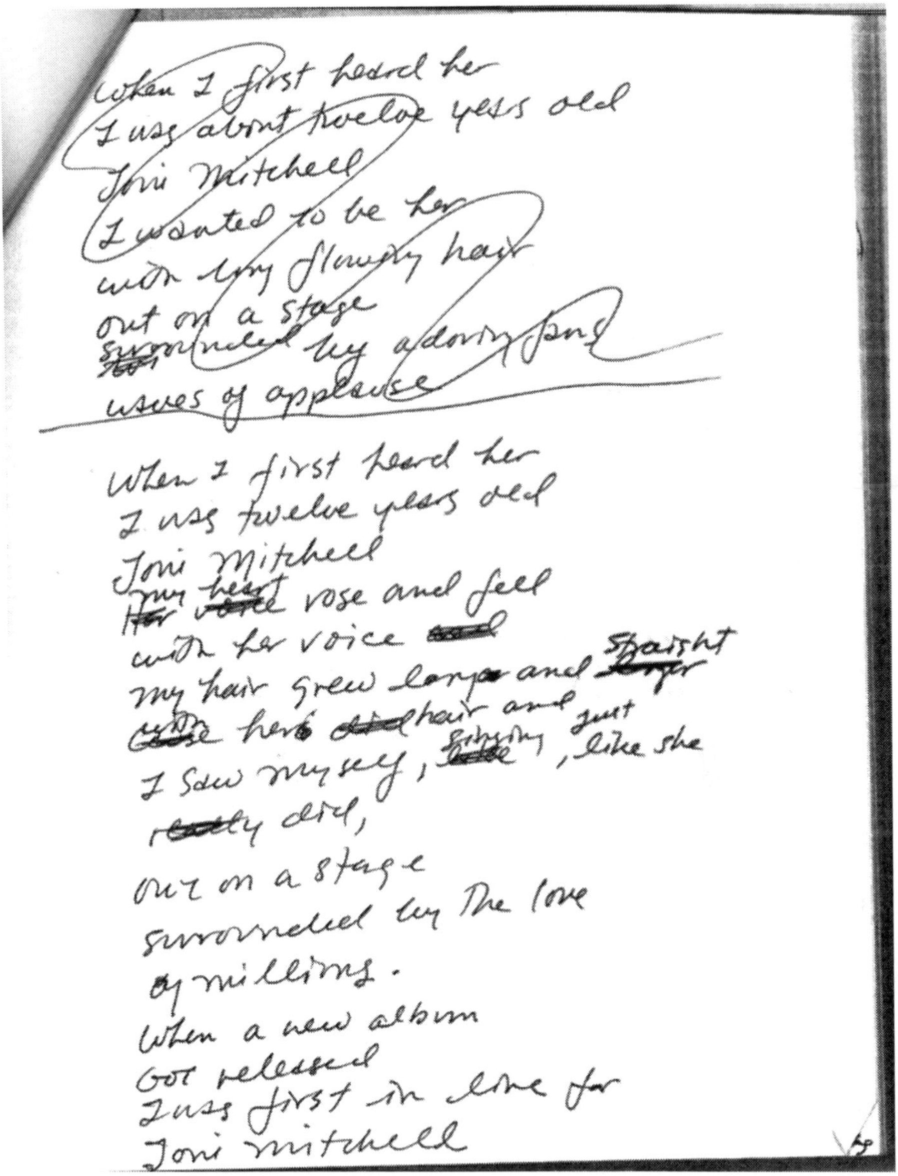

When I first heard her
I was about twelve years old
Joni Mitchell
I wanted to be her
with long flowing hair
out on a stage
surrounded by adoring fans
waves of applause

When I first heard her
I was twelve years old
Joni Mitchell
~~Her voice~~ my heart rose and fell
with her voice
my hair grew long and ~~longer~~ straight
~~Close~~ with her hair and
I saw myself, singing, just like she
~~really~~ did,
out on a stage
surrounded by the love
of millions.
When a new album
got released
I was first in line for
Joni Mitchell

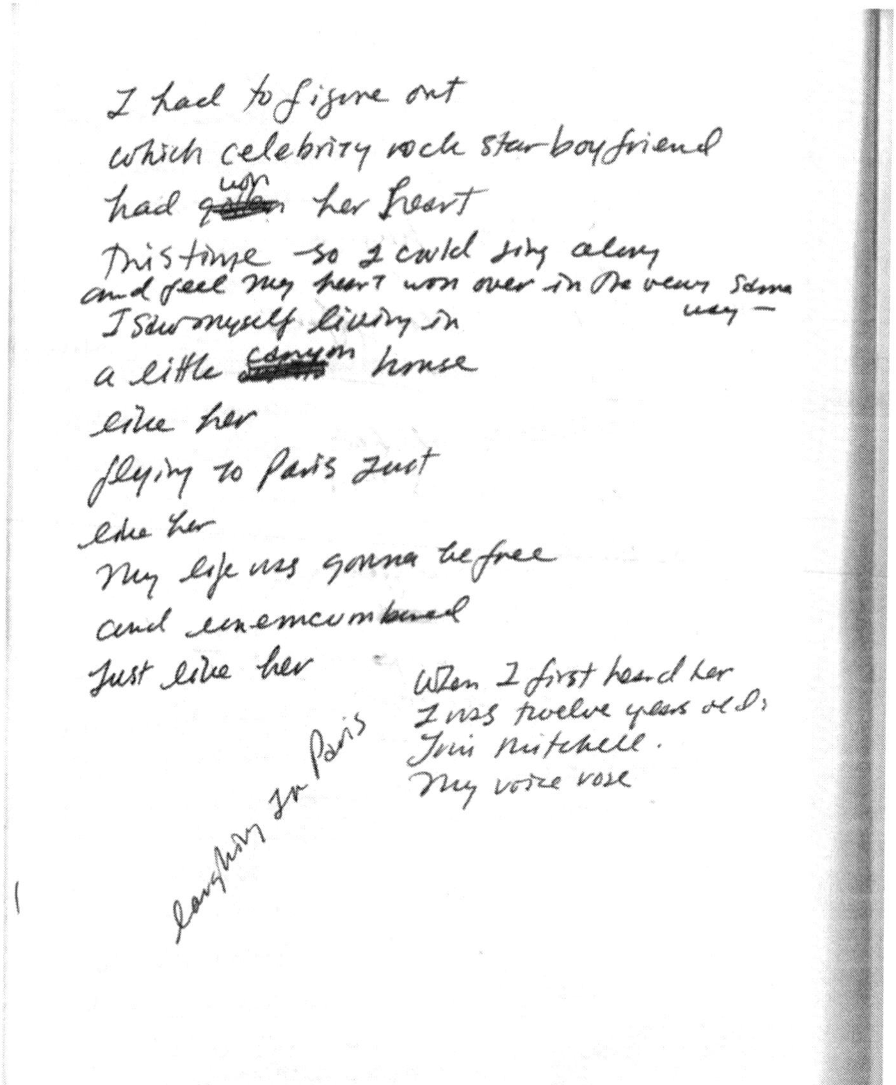

I had to figure out
which celebrity rock star boyfriend
had ~~gotten~~ won her heart
this time so I could sing along
and feel my heart won over in the very same way —
I saw myself living in
a little ~~[illegible]~~ canyon house
like her
flying to Paris just
like her
My life was gonna be free
and unencumbered
Just like her

When I first heard her
I was twelve years old,
Joni Mitchell.
My voice rose

laughing in Paris

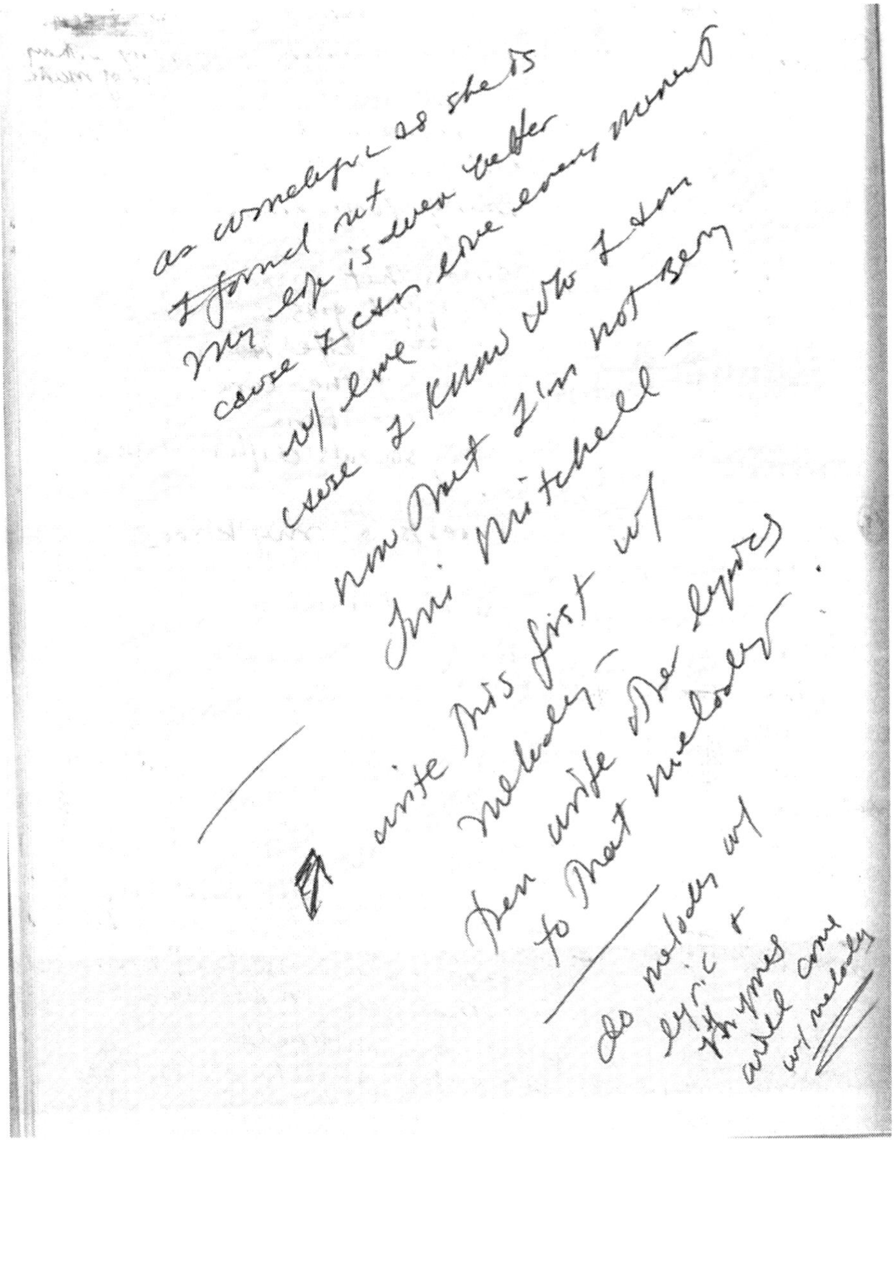
as complex as she is
I found out
my life is ever better
cause I can love every moment
w/ love
cause I know who I am
now that I'm not being
Joni Mitchell —
w/
write this first w/
melody — then lyrics
write the
then
to that melody
w/
do melody w/
lyric +
rhymes
will come
w/ melody

When I first heard her
I was 12 years old
Joni Mitchell, Joni Mitchell
My voice rose up
Just like her voice
Joni Mitchell, Joni Mitchell
I was reaching for her star
So I picked up my guitar
But I didn't realize
I was not being Joni Mitchell.

I was first in line for
Each new release of
Joni Mitchell, Joni Mitchell.
And my heart broke
Just like her heart
Joni Mitchell, Joni Mitchell
Life was new & I was bold
I was 18 years old
And I thought I couldn't live
If I was not being Joni Mitchell.

all the demoes that I made
All the late night gigs I played
Didn't send her life my way
Somewhere there were lessons learned
My road took another turn
& Everything looks different
to me now —

My first born child rests
upon my knee
and we rock sweetly, we rock sweetly
And as I sing out
~~Just like she sings out~~ (the way I sing out)
we get sleepy, very sleepy
~~Cause~~ and As fine as Joni stands —
I have found out who I am —
Now I'm loving every day
'Cause I'm not being Joni Mitchell —
No, I'm not being Joni Mitchell.

Not Being Joni Mitchell

When I first heard her
I was twelve years old
Joni Mitchell, Joni Mitchell
My voice rose up
Just like her voice
Joni Mitchell, Joni Mitchell
I was reaching for her star
So I picked up my guitar
But I didn't realize I was
Not being Joni Mitchell.

I was first in line for
Each new release of
Joni Mitchell, Joni Mitchell
And my heart broke
Just like her heart
Joni Mitchell, Joni Mitchell
I was young and I was bold
I was eighteen years old
And I thought I couldn't live if I was
Not being Joni Mitchell

All the demos that I made
All the late-night gigs I played
Didn't send her life my way
Somewhere there were lessons learned
My road took another turn
And everything looks different to me now

My firstborn child rests
Upon my knee and
We rock sweetly, we rock sweetly

And as I sing out
The way I sing out
We get sleepy, very sleepy
And as fine as Joni stands
I have found out who I am
Now I'm loving every day cause I'm
Not being Joni Mitchell—oh—no I'm
Not being Joni Mitchell.

9
CREATING LEAD SHEETS

"My songs are basically my diaries. Some of my best songwriting has come out of time when I've been going through a personal nightmare."
—Gwen Stefani

"For a songwriter, you don't really go to songwriting school. You learn by listening to tunes, and you try to understand them and take them apart and see what they're made of, and you wonder if you can make one, too."
—Tom Waits

You can have a lot of fun making your own lead sheets. It's also great to know how to notate your own music.

What are some advantages to knowing how to make your own lead sheets?

1. If you decide to put a band together, or just play with some other musicians, you've already got your own material written out for everyone—exactly the way you want it played.

2. After you complete your lead sheet, you can make copies of your music for everyone to learn and to use—at rehearsals, for fun, and to prepare for performances.

3. You will have a permanent record of your song so that you can always remember it.

4. You can also use a copy of this lead sheet for copyright purposes.

   For more information on copyrights, go to:

   http://www.copyright.gov/

   For an example of a copyright form from the United States Copyright Office, go to:

   http://www.copyright.gov/forms/formpa.pdf

5. You are not dependent on anyone else to do this for you!

You can start by writing music out by hand on manuscript paper. You can also input your music into a music notation program such as Finale or Sibelius. You can even draw or paint your own lead sheet cover if you want to get really artistic with it! This skill takes time to learn. Enjoy the process.

I think it's nice to know how to notate music by hand. The notation programs will put all your stems going in the correct directions and do everything for you, however, it's great to know the rules of music notation without the use of programs. You might be out somewhere, without an iPad or computer, and get an idea for a song! It's ideal to know how to jot things down correctly. You can always input your material into a program later for a great, professional-looking lead sheet.

When your music is written down, it can be read, understood, interpreted, and played by musicians. In order to make this possible, we have a system of notation that tells the musicians all of the information they need in order to perform the music that you, the songwriter, have in mind.

Here are some basic rules of music notation:

1. The *staff* is where we place our notes. It has five lines and four spaces.

The Staff

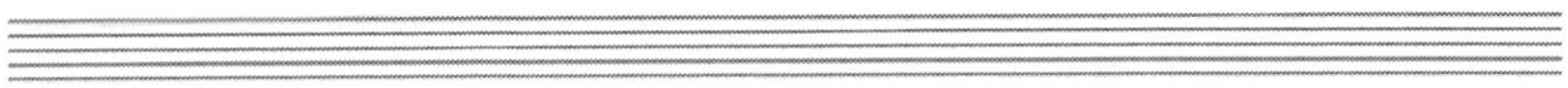

2. The *treble clef* and *bass clef* are commonly used in creating lead sheets. There are a number of different clefs used in music notation, however, for our purposes we will use these two clefs. The treble clef is also called the *G Clef* because it curls around the G line. The bass clef is also called the *F Clef* because the two little dots are on either side of the F line.

   The first (bottom) line of the treble clef is E and each space and line following that is the next letter of the alphabet.

   (We can also remember the lines as: Every Good Bird Does Fly and the spaces as spelling the word FACE: F, A, C, E)

The Treble Clef

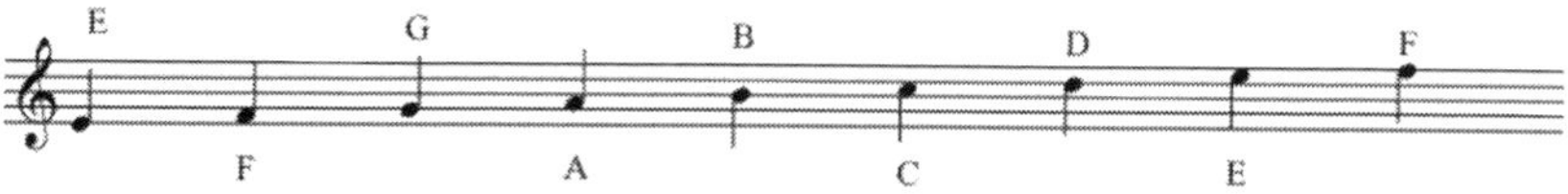

The bottom line of the bass clef is G, and each space and line following that is the next letter of the alphabet.

(We can also remember the lines as: Great Big Dogs Fight Animals and the spaces as: All Cars Eat Gas!)

The Bass Clef

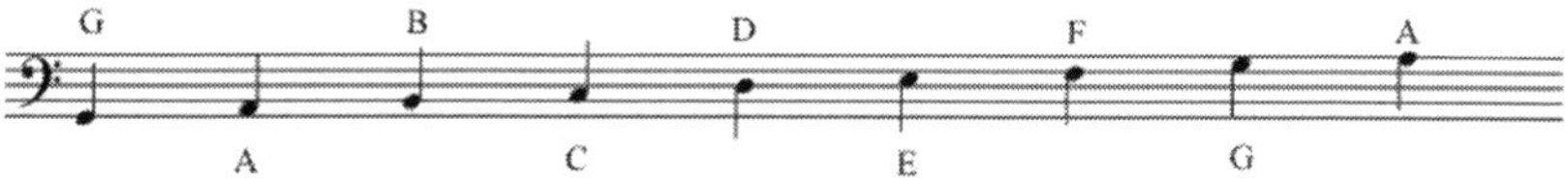

3. The *notes* or *pitches* are named with letters of the alphabet. The musical alphabet is A, B, C, D, E, F, and G. After G, we start over with A again. Every line or space on the staff stands for a different note/pitch. As we go up the staff, the notes ascend higher and vice versa.

   The notes are written by drawing little ovals on the lines, or in the spaces between the lines.

4. *Stems* on notes that are above the middle line go down, from the left side of the note. Stems on notes that are below the middle line, go up on the right side of the note. The size of the note-stems are normally one octave long.

Notes With Stems

5. *Accidentals* will raise or lower a note by a half step. A sharp will raise the note a half step and a flat will lower the note by a half step. A natural sign returns the note to the normal pitch and cancels any previous sharps or flats.

Accidentals

6. When we connect the treble and bass clefs together with a bracket or brace, it creates what we call a *grand staff.* The grand staff is often used to create lead sheets for piano/vocals. This makes it possible to increase the ranges of the notes that we can write down. Since the piano has a very wide range, the grand

staff works really well. We can put the vocal line on another staff, above the piano part.

We can also make a lead sheet for the melody only, using one staff line with chords above the notes and lyrics below. These kinds of lead sheets are often seen in "Fake Books"—big books with loads of songs in them. Fake Books are great for doing gigs, like weddings and parties, where people are requesting to hear all kinds of songs. Bring a Fake Book with you, and you'll be ready to read and play as you go!

Here are a few measures from a lead sheet I created using one staff for vocals, lyrics, and chords. I used slashes in the first four bars to notate the chords (four beats in each bar) before the vocal starts in the verse.

7. *Measures* (also called "bars") are used to organize the music. The lines that go down vertically on the staff divide the music up into organized sections. We mark the end of a piece of music with a double bar line in which the second line is bold (for the final bar line).

Measures

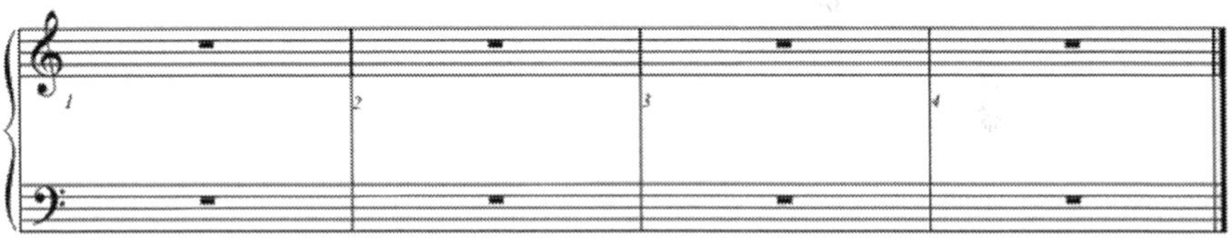

8. *Ledger lines* can be added above or below the staff. This makes it possible for lower or higher notes to be exhibited because they cannot fit on the staff.

   We can think of ledger lines as extra lines and spaces on the ends of the staff. Stems of ledger line notes go up or down toward the middle line.

Ledger Lines

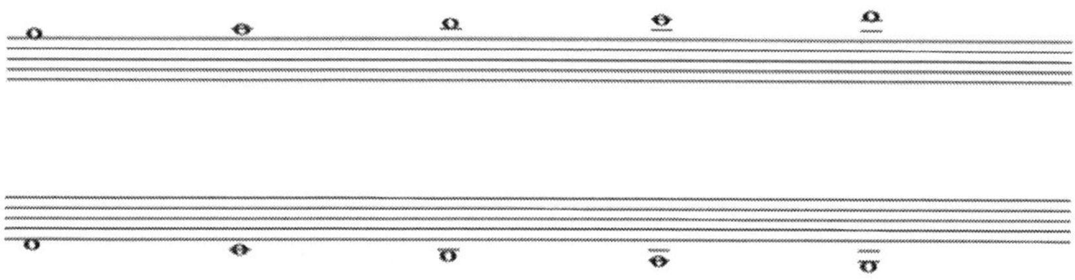

9. The length that a note is held is the note's *duration*. A whole note is equal to two half notes. A half note is equal to two quarter notes. A quarter note is equal to two eight notes, and an eighth note is equal to two sixteenth notes, and so on.

Duration Of Notes

Here is a picture of a "pyramid" of note values

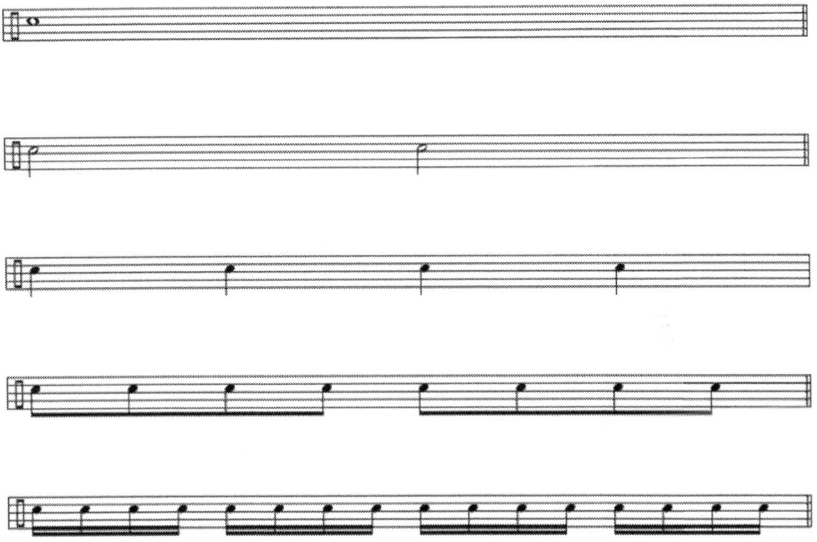

A dot next to a note adds to the duration of the note by half of the note's value.

Dotted Notes

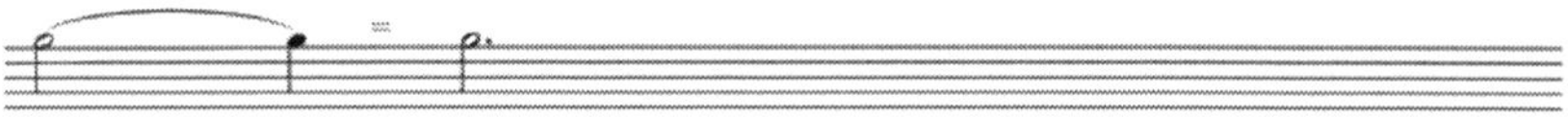

10. *Rests* indicate where the musician or singer does not play or sing. The length of a rest corresponds to the same values that we have for the duration of notes. So, we have whole rests, half rests, quarter rests, eighth rests, sixteenth rests, and so on.

Notes & Corresponding Rests

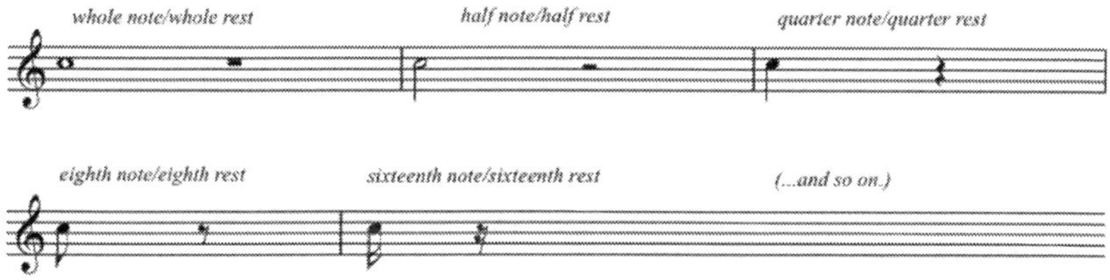

11. *Ties* connect two notes of the same pitch together. This lengthens the duration of the note.

Ties

12. The *time signature* tells us how many beats are in each measure and what kind of note gets one beat. The top number tells us how many beats there are in each measure (or bar). The bottom number tells us what note gets the beat.

For instance, in 4/4 we have four beats per bar and the quarter note gets one beat. In 6/8 time, we have six beats to the bar and the eighth note gets the beat.

Time Signature

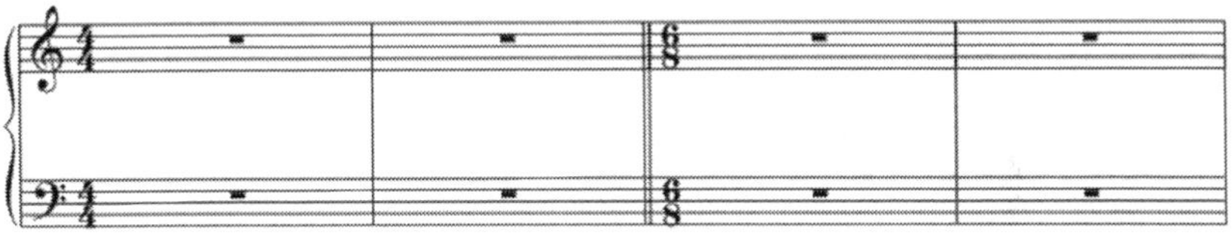

We can feel the beat, or pulse, of the music by clapping our hands or tapping our feet.

See if you can find the beat by clapping along to a favorite song. Listen to the bass and the drums especially. Try to determine what the time signature is.

13. *Repeats* tell us to go back and to repeat the music. We can have repeat signs at the beginning and at the end. This means that when we get to the second repeat sign, we go back to the first and repeat that section of music.

    Sometimes we can have a number of different endings. Repeat signs help us to notate verses and choruses with different lyrics and identical corresponding music and melodies.

14. *D.S.* stands for *Del Signo* and tells us to go to the sign. Many times you will see *D.S. al coda* or *D.S. al fine*. This tells us to go to

the sign and then from there, go to the coda or from there, go to the end.

15. When we get to the sign, we play to the end, to the coda, or to wherever the sign or the Del Signo tells us to go.

16. We also have a *coda sign.* The coda sign will tell us where to go for a special ending (the coda).

The Repeat, D.S. & Coda Signs

Depending upon your song's structure (ABAB, ABABCB, or AABA, etc.), you will have the use of repeat signs, D.S. al coda, D.S. al fine signs, and coda markings to help you convey to your musicians where to go.

These markings help to simplify the notation process. For example, in a song where the verse repeats twice and the chorus repeats three times, you have the use of the repeat and D.S. signs to help keep things a lot simpler.

Here are three examples of lead sheets I created for three of my own songs. You can see the differences between a piano/vocal lead sheet versus a lead sheet with a single staff that shows the melody, lyrics, and chords.

Repeats and signs help us create easy-to-read lead sheets with verses and choruses that have the same melodies and chords, yet different lyrics.

Every Living Thing Must Go

Words & Music by:
Lisa Donovan Lukas
(ASCAP)

2
Every Living Thing Must Go
Lisa Donovan Lukas
BRIDGE
F B♭ F B♭
Whis - per to - me - - - - in - side my dreams.
F B♭ F B♭
I will be list - en-ing to all - that you say - .
G C G C
You are - the wind that blows through the trees to
G C G F/G
tell me - you're wait 1. - ing to meet - me some-day - . 2.
VERSE
C F C F
Moth - er fath - er sis - ter friend - - - - . We
C F C F
leave the room - - - - - - Come back a gain - - - - . The
C F C F
fu - ture - is so long - - - - a - go - .
Am Am/G F C/E
Sum-mer comes to - bring the snow - Eve-ry liv - ing - thing must go -

Every Living Thing Must Go

Lisa Donovan Lukas

3

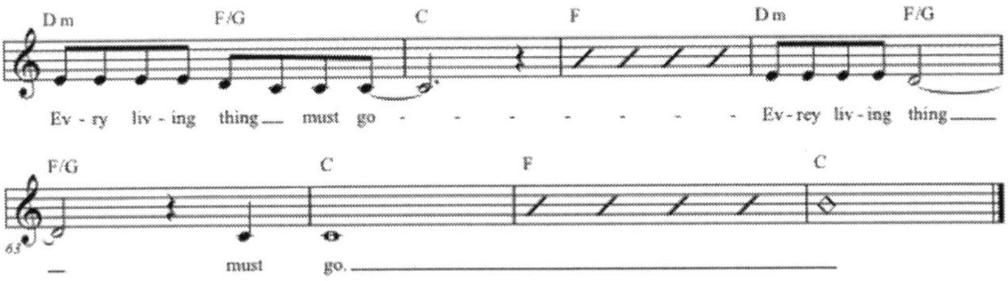

Like a Tree Stands Tall

(When the Tree Sings to The Girl &
The Girl Sings to The Tree)

Lisa Donovan Lukas

2
12
E♭(add2)
wind blown leaf. May-be you won-der how to stand your ground when the
love was a-round. Mu-sic and laugh-ter by the fire's light. With a
15
F
B♭
world you know. is up - side down. So ma - ny storms have come my
song and prayer to guide the night. I don't know how it is you
18
Gm7
way it's true. I've been torn in a mil - lion piec-es just like you.
do what you do. I on - ly know there's peace in look-ing at you.

3
21 E♭ F
Way down be - low me where no - one can see Hid - ing there's my
If I could real - ly take your place then would I feel your
24 B♭ F/E♭ E♭
re - ci - pe Just Put down some roots and
si - lent grace and
27 B♭/D Gm7 Cm7
stay a - while Have some pa - tience and

4
30 B♭/D
E♭(sus2)
F
faith and your own sweet smile
a lit - tle smile
33 B♭
F/E♭
B♭/D
Mix it to - geth - er with wa - ter and
36 Gm7
E♭
sun- shine
One morn - ing you'll wake up and
Would I real - ly wake up and

5
39 F(sus4) F B♭(sus4) B♭ B♭(sus2)
find that you're dif - ferent you're
that I'm dif - ferent I'm
p
mf
42 B♭ B♭(sus4)/A B♭(sus4)/G Gm7
strong - er you're green - er that's all, and you
strong - er I'm green - er that's all, if I
45 E♭ F(sus4) F E♭(sus2)
stand where you stand like a tree
stand where you stand

6
48
F
1.
B♭
stands
tall.
51
rit.
sim.
54
molto rit.
p

2.
7
57
B♭
D(sus4)
D7
Gm7
Cm7
tall.
Take a field of dais - ies
tall.
60
F
Fm7
B♭7
E♭
3
make it your own.
Grow ing and know-ing you'll stand on your own.
You'll
63
F
F7
B♭
F/E♭
E♭
make it a - lone, and Put down some roots and
and

8
66 B♭/D Gm7 Cm7
stay a - while. Have some pa - tience. and
69 B♭/D E♭(add2) F
faith and your own sweet smile
72 B♭ F/E♭ B♭/D
Mix it to - geth - er with wa - ter and

9
75 Gm7
Eb
sun- shine
One morn - ing you'll wake up and
78 F
Bb(sus4) Bb Bb(add2)
find
that you're dif - ferent you're
p
mf
81 Bb(add2) Bb Bb(sus4)/A Bb(sus4)/G Gm7
strong - er you're green - er that's all, and you

10
84
E♭
F(sus4)
F
E♭
F
stand where you stand like a tree stands
88
B♭
tall.
rit.
sim.
92
molto rit.
p

Lead Sheet

Not Being Joni Mitchell

Music & Lyrics by
Lisa Donovan Lukas

Not Being Joni Mitchell
2
E♭/F F7 B♭ E♭add2 B♭ E♭add2
Jo - ni Mitch-ell.
Verse 2
B♭ E♭add2 B♭ E♭add2
I was first in line for each new re - lease of Jo - ni
F/G Gm7 E♭/F F7
Mitch - ell, Jo - ni Mitch - ell.
B♭ E♭add2 B♭ E♭add2
and my heart broke, just like her heart, Jo - ni
F/G Gm7 E♭/F F7
Mitch - ell, Jo - ni Mitch - ell. I was
Gm7 E♭ B♭/D G♭
young and I was bold. I was eight-een years old,
Cm7 E♭/F Cm7
and I thought I could - n't live, if I was not be - ing
E♭/F F7 B♭ E♭add2 B♭ F/A
Jo - ni Mitch-ell.

Not Being Joni Mitchell
3
Bridge
Gm9 B♭6/D Gm9
All the dem - oes that I made all the late night
B♭6/D Gm9 E♭ Fsus
gigs I played, did - n't send her life my way.
F7 Gm9 B♭6/D Gm7
Some - where there were les - sons learned, My road took a -
Dm7 Gm7 E♭ Fsus F7
no - ther turn. Eve-ry thing looks dif-frent to me now. Oh.
B♭ E♭add2 B♭ E♭add2
Oh.
B♭ E♭add2 B♭ E♭add2
Verse 3
B♭ E♭add2 B♭
My first born child rests up - on my knee
E♭add2 F/G Gm7 E♭/F F7
and we rock sweet - ly, we rock sweet - ly.

Not Being Joni Mitchell

4

EXERCISE:

Go on a "field trip" to a local music store or an online music store. Spend some time browsing around in the sheet music section. Look at the difference between single piano/vocal sheet music for sale versus the music in compilation Fake Books.

Notice the format, the way the notes and lyrics are written, the time signatures, the chords, the repeat signs, codas, etc. Look at first and second endings and see how everything is laid out.

(An online store will sometimes show a sample of the first page only of the sheet music, so you will see more if you have the opportunity to look through entire pieces of music.)

My local music store is called Keyboard Concepts. They are terrific! Here are some online sites I frequent:

http://www.sheetmusicplus.com/welcome
http://www.musicnotes.com/
http://www.primamusic.com/
http://www.jwpepper.com/sheet-music/welcome.jsp

EXERCISE:

1. Choose one of your own songs.
2. Create a piano/vocal lead sheet using the grand staff for the piano part and a single staff above it for the vocal melody.
3. Make sure your stems are going in the correct direction.
4. Write the lyrics below each note on the vocal staff, and write the chords above the melody.

EXERCISE:

1. Choose one of your own songs.
2. Create a single-staff lead sheet with the melody written on the staff.
3. Make sure your stems are going in the correct direction.
4. Write the lyrics below each note, and write the chords above.

10

IN CONCLUSION

FINAL NOTES...

I believe that being alive means that we are always changing and growing. So, it's probably safe to say that I will never stop learning and wanting to learn. At least, that's my sincere intention. I think of my life, which includes my life as a musician, as an endless work in progress. I guess that's what keeps me forever fascinated with music, words, and creativity.

My hope is to get you started so that you'll never want to stop either. And maybe someday, you might even get the inkling to want to pass what you've learned on to the younger people you know—our next generation of music-makers, songwriters, and creators. Maybe some of these future music-makers will be your grandchildren or my great-grandchildren! Meanwhile, my wish is that you enjoy the process of learning about songwriting and all the creativity that comes with this most wonderful journey.

I have really loved writing *The Young Musician's Guide to Songwriting.* I hope you find it helpful and interesting.

With all my best wishes,

Lisa

11
ACKNOWLEDGMENTS

My teachers and guides—past, present, and future

My comrades and colleagues: fellow music teachers, troubadours, and musicians

My ever-encouraging and amazing kin: Erin Donovan

and

Centuries of epic songwriters

12
ABOUT THE AUTHOR

Lisa Donovan Lukas has worked as a songwriter, composer, pianist, vocalist, orchestrator, film and television music copyist/proofreader, and music teacher. Years of her music students' cumulative interest in writing and composing original material inspired her to create a guide to songwriting, specifically for young artists.

Lukas earned her Bachelor of Music degree in Composition from the USC Thornton School of Music and has been actively involved in the music industry ever since. Her songs have appeared in film and television, and Sheet Music Plus has published her educational piano music. Lukas's accolades include MTAC's prestigious Composers Today awards and numerous ASCAP Plus honors, including Popular Division and Concert Division awards.

Lukas is a member of the Music Teachers National Association and the Music Teachers' Association of California. She remains passionate about passing on the magical craft of songwriting to future generations.

For more information and to listen to some of Lisa's music, please visit:

http://www.lisadonovanlukas.com

32337900R00141

Made in the USA
Charleston, SC
15 August 2014